Ordinary Woman, Extraordinary God

To Lynda

Nothing is impossible!
(Jeremiah 32:27)
God bless you
Alison
- X -

Alison McLeod
with
Jan Levin

TEACH Services, Inc.
P U B L I S H I N G
www.TEACHServices.com • (800) 367-1844

Copyright © 2019 Alison McLeod

Copyright © 2019 TEACH Services, Inc.

ISBN-13: 978-1-4796-0980-2 (Paperback)

ISBN-13: 978-1-4796-0981-9 (ePub)

Library of Congress Control Number: 2018956825

TEACH Services, Inc.
P U B L I S H I N G
www.TEACHServices.com • (800) 367-1844

Disclaimer

Alison McLeod is not a physician. The following is simply the story of her medical journey and should not be construed as giving medical advice in any form. If you have medical problems of any kind, please see your healthcare professional for diagnosis, treatment, and advice.

Dedication

To Jesus, my Heavenly Husband, my Prince of Peace
"Whom have I in heaven but you? And I desire no one on earth as much as you! My health fails; my spirits droop, yet God remains! He is the strength of my heart; he is mine forever!"
(Psalm 73:25–26)
As the bow is unto the string
As the fingers to the keys
As the sunlight to the flower
As the breeze unto the trees
As the prince unto the maiden
As the hero to his love
So, Lord, are You to me.
(Alison McLeod, 2013)
"O Lord, I will honor and praise your name, for you are my God; you do such wonderful things! You planned them long ago, and now you have accomplished them, just as you said!"
(Isaiah 25:1)

Contents

A Word of Thanks

With heartfelt gratitude…

To **Jan**, my editor, for being the catalyst and my greatest cheerleader in the writing of this story. I could not have done it without you. It has been a privilege.

To **Dr. Todd Boren**, my skilled surgeon, for not giving up on me and for supporting me as I chose to swim upstream.

To **Dr. N**, my compassionate physician, for your tremendous encouragement and support as you allowed us both to be led by God through my recovery.

To **Mom and Dad**, for your unfailing love, prayers and e-mails that show me how much you care. You are my rock of support.

To my children, **Melissa, Kyle, and Daniel**, for loving me unconditionally. You are my treasure.

To my grandson, **Wesley**, for giving me a reason to live and to hope. You fill my heart with joy.

To **Richard and Jenny**, for sheltering my children and me through the storm and inspiring me with your faith. You sacrificed much.

To **Trevor and Colleen**, for being my family in a strange land, caring and supporting in countless ways. There are no words.

To **Taryn**, for being a nurse and a friend through my darkest hours and beyond. You stepped in when I had no one.

To **Dan and Ruth**, for your love in action with the supplements and teas, and for being such wonderful parents-in-law to my precious girl.

To **Johana**, for understanding me perfectly and never failing to say the right words to encourage me through my darkest days. Your friendship is a precious gift.

To **Uncle Fernando and Auntie Sara**, for lifting the burden of the medical bills and for being the best boss I ever had. Thank you for being my adopted parents!

To **Anelize**, for inspiring me with your own story. It gave me something to hold on to when the fear seemed overwhelming.

To **Jodi**, for being a faithful friend and for introducing me to Ruth Harms Calkin. Your visits in the hospital were a ray of sunshine.

To the **Wildwood staff and students**, for being an indispensable part of my healing process.

To **Melissa, Jenny, and Colleen**, for lending your writing and editing skills.

Prologue

**"For I am going to do something in your own lifetime
that you will have to see to believe."**

(Habakkuk 1:5)

On a glorious April day in 2016, in the heart of beautiful British Columbia, I gazed down at my brand-new grandson sleeping in my arms. My heart throbbed with wonder. I stroked his tiny fingers, and watched his chest rise and fall in gentle rhythm. He was perfect—his downy head, his little rosebud mouth, his miniature toes. Love filled my heart, and tears of gratitude welled up in my eyes. I remembered the day my daughter told me her happy news. How I pasted on a smile for her and her husband, then put down the phone and wept. How dread clutched at me and whispered that I would never live to meet my first grandchild. I shook my head, and cuddled little Wesley closer, marveling in the miracle of it all.

My thoughts traveled back over the past ten months to the diagnosis that hit me like a train, leaving me in a daze of fear, pain, and disbelief. The hospital, the surgery, the nightmare. The incredible chain of events that unfolded in the days that followed, days that I should not have lived. Now I sat holding a precious little boy I should never have seen, sharing a special time with my daughter and her family. I had been given a new life, a second chance. Could any soul be more blessed?

I want to share my journey with you. It's been a roller coaster of tears and laughter, despair and triumph. There are happy times, and terrible times. And there is always God, the One who has never failed me, and Who has taught me, through all the ups and downs, to cling tightly to Him no matter what life throws at me. This is a love story, tracing the thread of God's faithfulness throughout my life. He is taking me from brokenness to wholeness in every way, and this book is my love gift to Him.

He still performs miracles. I am one of them. Come with me to where it all began....

Chapter 1

Beginnings

"Teach a child to choose the right path, and when he is older, he will remain upon it."

(Proverbs 22:6)

On April 2, 1966, I entered the world two weeks early, in what people affectionately termed "the sleepy hollow" of Pietermaritzburg, South Africa. However, my arrival was anything but sleepy. My mom tells me that with her final push I shot out and the doctor caught me in mid-air! I had my guardian angel busy right from the start! With round, blue eyes and a shock of dark hair, I captured the hearts of my mom, dad, and grandparents, who were all in the delivery room. My parents named me after my mom's favorite actress, June Allyson, who played the part of Jo in the 1949 movie, *Little Women*. I inherited the looks and quiet reserve of my maternal grandmother and the introverted personality of my dad. The oldest daughter of four children, God blessed me with parents who loved me dearly.

On my first birthday, my dad penned a poem, referring to me as a small spark of twinkling mischief. He expressed regret that I would have to grow and learn to live apart from his protection. How we all long to gather our little ones under our wings and protect them from the hurts of life. But we live in a world controlled by the enemy, who had me in his sights from the very beginning. At eighteen months, I toppled off the kitchen table and split my chin open. I do not recall the incident but carry the scar from the stitches to this day. From those earliest moments God kept His hand over me. I could have been paralyzed for nobody at the hospital thought to check me thoroughly, but according to a chiropractor who took an x-ray in my twenties, I broke my neck. He marveled, "If it weren't for your strong shoulder and neck muscles, you would not be able to hold your head up straight." To this day I suffer with severe muscle tension and headaches from time to time but manage to function well despite my injury.

My mom recalls me as a quiet and sensitive child. "My pet name for you is 'gentle doe.' It showed in your expression. You had a softness in your eyes, like a little doe, innocent and trusting. You didn't like to see people or animals in pain or suffering. A deep thinker, you never talked much about your feelings. Sometimes you looked at me with a wise look beyond your age in maturity. You thought things through, and once you made a decision about something, you took it seriously."

Two sisters and a brother followed me in quick succession. As the first-born I developed a strong sense of responsibility and definite perfectionistic tendencies. In spite of the typical sibling squabbles, I felt like a mother hen if anyone from the "outside" dared to hurt one of us. I remember feeling particularly protective toward my little brother.

As a child I had a strong constitution and seldom felt sick. The usual childhood diseases didn't bother me. I contracted mild cases of the measles and whooping cough and then, unfortunately, passed them on to my poor siblings, who suffered far worse than I did. The chicken pox found me with only a few spots, while my sisters and brother were inundated! Perhaps God gifted me with an extra measure of vital force in preparation for what I would face in later years.

Starting school proved to be a traumatic experience, due to my young age and introverted personality. Three months before my sixth birthday, South African law required me to begin first grade. There I experienced bullying from one of the girls in my class at school. My personality is not naturally aggressive, and I did not know how to fight back. My tendency is to become paralyzed and simply allow life to happen to me. As we jostled for position on the story mat one morning, the bully punched me in the stomach, leaving me with an excruciating stomach-ache for the rest of the day. I never told anyone, but later that day my mom found me doubled over in my bedroom, crying in pain, and the story came out.

I didn't do well in first grade—neither socially nor academically—but learning to read opened up a whole new world for me. I had my nose in a book every chance I could get! In the second grade I exhausted the small library of books that the school kept for the lower grades. My eyes lit up the day my teacher decided to take me to the "big kid's library" to choose a book! The first book I borrowed told the story of a tiny princess named Rosebud who lived in a flower. My seven-year-old self felt very important to be the only one in my class allowed into the "big" library. I appreciate the fact that God instilled in me a love for reading and writing from a young age. It helped greatly as I attempted to write this book.

Religion played an important part in my life from the beginning. When my parents met, my mom was a Seventh-day Adventist, and my dad a Methodist. My dad smoked a pipe, but kicked the habit with alacrity when my mom told him she could never marry a man who smoked! He had planned to become a Methodist minister, but after they married he began to study the Adventist faith. My dad decided to be baptized into the church when I was two years old.

I grew up in an era when the church in general tended to be legalistic. I heard plenty about the do's and don'ts, but not much about how to have a real connection with Jesus. Being a perfectionist and a people-pleaser, I felt pressure to be obedient and suffered with guilt when I could not be as perfect as I thought I should be.

However, I learned valuable lessons from an early age. My parents believed that actions should have consequences. One sweltering South African summer day, a neighbor friend and I played together outside. Suddenly we heard the music from an ice-cream van a few streets away. The thought of a delicious, cold ice-cream appealed to two hot and thirsty little girls. My parents limited our consumption of sweets and desserts, so I knew my mom wouldn't give us money for ice-cream. I suggested to my friend, "Let's ask your mom." My friend, being too afraid, replied, "You ask her." Unbelievably, considering my shyness, I marched boldly up to the neighbor's house and before I knew it, out of my mouth came a lie: "My mom wants to buy ice cream, but doesn't have any cash. Can she borrow some from you?" The neighbor gladly gave me the money. My friend and I sat on the curb to wait for the ice cream van, but it never came down our street that day. My mom found me with the money still clutched in my hand. "Where did you get that?" I had no choice but to confess. As punishment I had to go and apologize to the neighbor lady and return her money. My whole body burned with shame. While a hard lesson to learn, it taught me much about respect and honesty.

In my tenth year, I began to struggle with emotional eating and many other devastating issues. Circumstances in my life at that time caused me to feel insecure. My four-year-old brother required a great deal of my mom's attention and I felt left out. I didn't express my feelings easily, so my parents found it difficult to read my heart. Vulnerable, I looked for attention and affirmation. A family friend took advantage of this and molested me on a number of occasions. I felt ashamed and, unfortunately, did not tell anyone. I began experiencing debilitating migraine headaches. These were most likely related to my neck injury as a baby. However, the stress of the abuse I had suffered and my inability to express myself were probably a major contributing factor. In the midst of this, my dad became ill with jaundice. Being a sensitive child, I worried about him. I turned to food for comfort, and my old problem with dishonesty resurfaced.

Our dietary restrictions never bothered me until this difficult period, when I started craving sweet things. During my dad's illness, I sneaked Jell-O® powder from the kitchen cupboard and hid away behind the sofa to eat it. When my mom discovered the theft, I felt a deep sense of shame, especially when she lamented, "I have been saving that Jell-O® powder to make for your dad, who is feeling so sick." However, the compulsion to comfort myself with food continued. I discovered a slab of chocolate in my mom's bedroom cupboard and decided to help myself to some. But I took too much and my mom found out. More shame!

Not an independent child, I felt both brave and guilty the day I took the little money that I had and rode my bicycle to the store a few blocks away. I had never ventured this far from home alone before. I bought a large slab of white milk chocolate and, after arriving home, hid in my bedroom and ate the whole thing!

Our family became vegetarian around this time, and I had strong cravings for the meat I used to love. At Christmastime we usually got together with my mom's family. We always had a traditional dinner with a roast turkey and all the trimmings. This particular Christmas I crept into the kitchen after dinner and sneaked some turkey! My mom would probably have given me some if I asked for it, but being a timid child, I did not have the courage to ask.

My mom was an excellent cook, and we were active children with healthy appetites. Eating became an important part of my life and I over-ate regularly. I seemed to have a fast metabolism because I somehow remained skinny. However, these patterns of emotional eating became entrenched and I struggled with them for many years to come.

Over time I learned more about God, and at the age of twelve felt inspired and convicted to be baptized. My best friend had been asking me for some time to be baptized with her, but I had resisted. My mom taught my Sabbath School class, and each week she used the flannel board to share with us a chapter in the life of Ellen White. One Sabbath the story of young Ellen's surrender to Christ and her baptism touched me, and I decided on impulse to join my friend in preparing for baptism. Although I did not have a personal relationship with Jesus, I was sensitive to spiritual things. We chose August 5, 1978, to be baptized together. I don't think the enemy liked this, for the night before the baptism, the water heater started a fire and burned the baptistry down! Thankfully an alternative venue became available, and the baptism went ahead. On that chilly August afternoon, as the pastor lowered me under the water, I'm sure I didn't understand the full implications of my decision. But I believe I became God's girl from that day on. Even though I never found a real connection with Him until much later in my life, He kept His hand over me and never left my side.

After my baptism, I tried to be a good girl and read my Bible every night, but it didn't mean much to me and I felt guilty when, at the age of fourteen, I decided to stop reading it altogether. I attended the Adventist school on the campus where we lived, and where my dad served as the music teacher. We went to the campus church and joined in all the spiritual activities. We had regular family worship. But I passed through my teenage years never learning how to surrender my heart to Christ. Feeling empty and insecure, I welcomed the attention of boys, only to push them away when they became too serious.

As a young teenager, my interest in health and taking care of my body began to grow. Ever since our family became vegetarian we maintained a fairly healthy lifestyle. Unfortunately, in my sixteenth year, my mom

As a young teenager, my interest in health and taking care of my body began to grow.

received the dreaded diagnosis of ovarian cancer. Our lives were thrown into turmoil. My mom had surgery, followed by monthly chemotherapy treatments for a year. Eventually the doctors stopped the treatment as they could see it was killing her. At first I felt detached and numb. My relationship with my mom had faltered as I entered my teen years. Not a rebellious teenager on the outside, I did experience rebellious feelings at times. I had a strong sense of responsibility and didn't like to break any rules, so I never acted out, but on the inside I struggled. Without Jesus in my heart I grew to be a selfish young person. Although I felt disconnected from my mom, I couldn't bear to see her suffering. The sound of her vomiting tormented me, but I didn't know how to help her. I endured each day at school like a robot. When I came home I helped to serve the meals that our neighbors kindly provided. The dark cloud of illness hung over our home and dampened our spirits.

As my mom slowly recovered from the chemotherapy, my parents made many changes in their diet, eventually becoming vegan. Their example of faithfulness to a healthy lifestyle made a huge impact on my life—even though I didn't embrace it fully myself until much later. During this time my mom's relationship with God grew immensely. One evening, as a group of friends prayed in a circle with her, she sensed the presence of angels and felt a warm sensation coursing through her whole body. She seemed to hear God say to her, "You are going to be fine." From that time on she began to get well, and by God's grace, my mom is a cancer survivor. However, the side effects of the chemotherapy still haunt her to this day. As a result of her experience, she has been able to understand and encourage me in my own health battles.

In spite of the trauma of my mom's illness, I maintained good grades at school, and passed my final exams with no trouble. At the age of seventeen I left home to attend college, more than eight hundred miles away. I felt apprehensive about being on my own for the first time in my life. However, I attended a conservative Seventh-day Adventist college, Helderberg College, in Somerset West, South Africa, and soon learned to love being there. I studied diligently, worked hard in the cafeteria and the music department for a student scholarship, and enjoyed fun times with my friends. Surrounded by mountains and ocean, I had the privilege of living in one of the most beautiful spots in South Africa. But I still felt an inexplicable emptiness inside of me. I searched for a relationship with Jesus but didn't know how to find it.

Taking a walk up on the mountain one day, I had a long talk with God, giving myself to Him as best I knew how. I felt a peace, but didn't understand that faith is more than just a feeling. After a few days the feeling disappeared, and I decided that this God stuff didn't work. I thought that since I felt nothing, I had no real connection with Christ, and God didn't care about me. I did not grasp what it means to live by faith and to surrender my heart on a daily, moment-by-moment basis. I continued with the busyness of college life and tried to ignore the ache in my heart.

But God stayed close to me. I loved music and when a few other students asked me to form a singing group with them, I gladly accepted. One evening we gave a concert at a church nearby. On the freeway on the way back, one of the car tires had a blowout. The car spun out of control, went off the road, through a fence, and into a ditch. As we spun in a circle I felt as though we were in slow motion. It seemed to take forever to make that loop before we shot off the road. I sat in the front seat without a seatbelt, yet none of us suffered any injury. Miraculously there were no other cars on the road at that time. The angels protected us that night.

By the time I reached college-age, my overeating caught up with me and I began to gain weight. Being part of a large family, we could never afford to eat out at restaurants often. In college things were different, and I frequently ate out with my friends. I discovered that this fueled my eating addiction. The college cafeteria did not serve meat, but I began to have meat when I ate out, although I knew it wasn't the best thing for me. From this point on I struggled with emotional eating and even though I could lose weight at times, the weight would creep back on again.

While in college, at the age of nineteen, I started dating my husband-to-be. Two-and-a-half years older than me, he had the reputation of being a rebel. Flattered that he seemed interested in me, I allowed him to sweep me off my feet in no time. I fell deeply in love with him and within three months we were engaged. But I did not seek my parents' counsel, as they were far away, nor did I consult God about this important decision. Looking back, I recognize that my youth and immaturity—and the rosy-tinted glasses of love—prevented me from paying attention to the obvious warning signs.

My fiancé and I graduated together—he with a bachelor's in business administration, and me with a secretarial diploma. After graduation my fiancé left to do his compulsory two years of military service, required by all white young men in South Africa at that time. I stayed at college for a further six months to complete a few additional secretarial courses. We missed each other desperately, and countless letters and phone calls crossed the miles separating us.

My fiancé's basic training base was located not too far from where my parents lived. When I went home from college for that Easter vacation we were able to spend some time together. His parents lived several hours away and we decided to take a trip to visit them. On this trip I experienced God's intervention in my life in an unmistakable way.

My fiancé offered to give an army friend a ride to his home, not far from where we were headed. We left my parents' home at around 10:00 p.m., a mistake, for both men were sleep-deprived as a result of their rigorous training in the army camp. The army friend passed out in the back seat, and I did not have a driver's license, so my fiancé had to drive. As the night wore on his eyelids began to droop and every now and then the car wandered off the road. I panicked, believing that we were going to have an accident and be killed! I began to pray as I had never prayed in my life before, desperately pleading with God to keep my fiancé awake and to spare our lives. Suddenly the car began to jerk violently—so violently that it became impossible for *anyone* to sleep! In South Africa it is dangerous to stop on the road at night, and being in the middle of nowhere, we had to keep going. The car jerked all the way to my fiancé's parents' house, and as a result he did not fall asleep once! We worried that something serious had gone wrong with the car and that it would be expensive to fix. The next day a mechanic came to take a look at it. After a few minutes he reported, "It's just a wire that pulled loose. Your car is fine."

I am sure God sent an angel to loosen that wire in answer to my prayer! I am struck by the tender, faithful way my God always deals with me. Even though I wasn't walking with Him as I should have been at that time, He did not hesitate to answer my desperate prayer.

Chapter 2

Happiness and Heartache

**"Can a mother forget her little child and not have love for her own son?
Yet even if that should be, I will not forget you."**

(Isaiah 49:15)

My fiancé and I were married towards the end of his first year in the
military. I believed in fairy tale marriages and felt sure that I had found
the one who would fill the aching void in my life. For my new husband's
second year of military service he transferred to Cape Town, a large city
near the college where we had studied. We rented an apartment on the
college campus, and I found employment in the college business office.
I loved being married and setting up our little nest. Never an ambitious
career woman, my dreams of being a wife, and hopefully soon a mother,
were coming true.

However, cracks soon began to show. I had unrealistic expectations
about marriage and how my husband should treat me. When problems
arose, my introvert nature drove me to avoid confrontation, and feeling
hurt, I withdrew. My discontent, silence, and emotional retreat were ugly
and dishonoring to God. Not long after we were married I stopped attending church regularly. I needed to find the meaning for myself regarding
the religion I had been raised in. Since I didn't know Jesus, I felt like

a hypocrite each week attending church. It came a little late, but I had entered the "rebellious" years of my life.

When we weren't working, my husband and I spent time with friends at the beach, going to the movies, and eating out. I used my "addictions"—to my husband, food, and now movies, too—to try to combat the emptiness I still felt. I longed for my husband to meet the needs that I now realize only Jesus could fill. We didn't see much of each other during the week, and when he occasionally spent hours out fishing with his friends on a Sunday, I felt abandoned. In my mind, he didn't spend enough meaningful time with me. I made my husband my whole world, but the feeling did not seem to be mutual. To top it all, my insecurity haunted me every time I felt that he had been over-familiar with another woman. Not a recipe for a happy marriage!

After my marriage, the comfort-eating patterns that I struggled with since childhood continued. I became desperate at times, feeling out of control. I hated being overweight, yet seemed powerless to stop finding comfort in food. It seemed to be the only way I could cope with my emotions. Eating and losing weight became an obsession with me. The enemy had me securely bound in his web of this love-hate relationship with food.

My husband and I waited four years before deciding to have a baby. Our perfect baby girl, Melissa, made her appearance without a sound, after a difficult forceps delivery. We decided that I would be a stay-at-home mom, and I loved taking care of my little girl. I wrote in my journal, "She's an absolute delight!" We spent our days together doing the chores around the house, taking walks in the sunshine, and reading stories together. However, my husband kept busy and I missed adult company. I battled with loneliness. This only compounded my problems with comfort eating. After Melissa was born we began attending church regularly again because we wanted to take our baby to Sabbath School. However, I still had not found my own personal walk with God. I went through the motions, but my heart wasn't in it.

Two-and-a-half years later, our precious son, Kyle, arrived, yelling lustily until he felt secure wrapped in a soft blanket and laid next to my head. Melissa, not quite three, loved her little brother dearly. When I took Kyle for his immunizations at the baby clinic, Melissa stood with her hands over her ears screaming! When questioned, "Why are you screaming?" she wailed, "I'm crying for my brother!" I loved being a mom. My journal entry when Kyle was two months old reads, "I didn't think I could love my little boy so much!" But I found it difficult adjusting to having two children. Melissa had been an easy baby, but Kyle had colic and didn't sleep well. I felt tired all the time. He demanded a great deal of my attention and Melissa found this difficult since she still needed me too.

When Kyle was eight months old, I became pregnant again. This was unexpected, but not unwelcome. I never regretted it for a moment. At twelve weeks pregnant, my journal records, "I want this baby so much!" Christopher arrived just seventeen months after his older brother. Both Kyle and Christopher were born by C-section—a breeze compared to Melissa's difficult delivery. Christopher also struggled with colic and sleeping at night. As much as I loved my precious babies, I often felt over-whelmed. Comfort eating wrapped itself around me and I began to gain weight. Pregnancy and breastfeeding had been a time of unrestrained eating, as I could eat as much as I wanted and not gain weight. But as soon as I stopped breastfeeding the weight returned. The cracks in my marriage began to widen. I feared that my husband did not find me beautiful any-more and my self-esteem plummeted. It became a vicious cycle: the worse I felt, the more I ate, which made me feel even worse. Without God in my life I saw myself as a woman of no worth.

Towards the end of 1998, my husband and I heard about a satellite evangelism series to be held at our church. We both felt impressed to attend—perhaps mostly for the novelty of attending a satellite broadcast from America—but I believe the Holy Spirit moved upon our hearts. I still had a huge, empty hole in my life, and when evangelist-pastor Dwight Nelson presented Jesus as our "Forever Friend," I felt drawn to Him. Both my husband and I experienced a spiritual revival, and a desire to give our lives to Jesus. We began keeping prayer journals and seeking God's will for our future.

Around this time we visited with some friends from our college days who had just returned from teaching English in South Korea. They were recruiting English teachers for the language schools operated by the Adventist church there. We were intrigued and drawn to the idea of being missionaries to Korea. We desired to do something meaningful with our lives, and this seemed like the perfect opportunity. We applied and were accepted. Plans were made to get passports and begin the process of pack-ing up our lives in South Africa. We decided to sell our house and most of our possessions and dedicate a good few years of our lives to working in Korea. However, the enemy didn't like this, and struck with a vengeance.

On New Year's Day, 1999, my husband decided to confess to me an affair he had two years previous. I appreciated that he wanted to "come clean" with me, but my world shattered into a million pieces. I forgave him instantly. However, my mind struggled to accept it. This wasn't supposed to happen. Driving in my car, I pounded the steering wheel and cried out, "Why, Lord, why?!" As I sobbed out my anguish in the shower one morning, my husband came in and held me. But I could not find comfort. Before I even began to process this tragedy, the enemy struck again. This time he targeted our youngest son.

Chapter 3
Chrissie

"You have collected all my tears and preserved them in your bottle!"

(Psalm 56:8)

Christopher arrived early on May 5, 1995. Chrissie (as he soon became known) didn't look much like our other two children at all. With his mother's chin, he definitely favored my side of the family, causing my husband to remark in the delivery room, "This is a Livingstone baby!" In spite of battling colic at night, Chrissie turned out to be placid and content during the day, with the exception of bath time, which he screamed his way through. He loved feeling warm and cozy and hated being undressed. Melissa and Kyle adored their new baby brother and couldn't stop touching him. Melissa's sweet four-year-old face, cheeks sucked in, hovered over him as she lovingly patted his tiny hands. Kyle, at a robust seventeen months, had a tendency to grab and I watched him carefully. We felt blessed with our three beautiful, healthy children.

For the first two years of Chrissie's life, we lived on a rural college campus, and were privileged to have my parents living just down the road from us. My mom recalls how Chrissie made his way over to their house to visit. He probably knocked, but she didn't hear it. Walking into the kitchen, she saw a small blurred figure through the glass door, sitting on their steps. My mom opened the door and sat down beside him. "Hello

Chrissie." Sitting there peacefully together, they watched the world go by. A contemplative child, Chrissie often sat in this way, quietly observing all the activities happening around him. At other times, he loved being a clown and making his sister and brother laugh.

Soon after Chrissie turned two, we moved back to a small duplex that we owned in Gordon's Bay, South Africa. I loved this home, so close to the ocean and the mountains that I could almost touch them. The three children shared a bedroom—Melissa and Kyle in the bunk bed, and Chrissie in his wooden bed tucked away in the corner. Chrissie imitated everything his brother and sister did, and they all sat and "read" story books together in their beds before going to sleep at night. When it came time for lights-out I loved the feel of Chrissie's chubby arms around my neck and kisses from his funny little mouth. He always had at least five different toys in the bed with him, and we were in trouble if any of them fell out during the night!

Chrissie's favorite time with his daddy became the early mornings. He crawled into bed with my husband and lay there as quiet as a mouse. Woe betide anyone who presumed to lie in *his* place! He carried a square cloth diaper (which he called his "nanum") around with him constantly, and this had to be tucked in next to his face in the bed.

I have many precious snapshots in my mind: Kyle and Chrissie sitting peacefully together, building with their Duplo® blocks; Chrissie laughing hysterically at a silly game he and Kyle were playing; Chrissie concentrating on his kindergarten game on the computer—an expert with that mouse! I picture all three children sitting at the kitchen deck eating their meals, Chrissie asking for the "cloffie" and constantly wiping his mouth. He hated getting any food on his face. He loved muesli and ate it for breakfast and supper. His other favorites included avocado on toast, scrambled eggs, and oatmeal.

I loved watching Chrissie at the beach. His toddler figure with knees that turned slightly in made me smile. He never ventured into the icy Atlantic Ocean waves like Melissa and Kyle, but stayed on the edge of the water. He always felt cold before his brother and sister and came and sat near me, wrapped in a towel, to play contentedly in the white sand.

Chrissie had twinkling blue eyes and straight, blonde hair, which kinked into a cow-lick in the front, just like his mother. Dimples peeped out when he smiled, and his delightful giggle brought joy to my heart. His curly mouth fascinated me, as it moved constantly. He wasn't a beautiful child as Kyle had been at his age, but he had a cute, intriguing little face that you could not stop looking at. A happy child, Chrissie laughed often and could be affectionate if he chose. When he felt ready, he came and flung his arms around my legs, exclaiming "Mama!" with adoration in his voice. However, at other times, if he didn't feel like giving you a hug right then, you could forget it! His stubbornness drove us crazy! When he learned to tie his own shoelaces, we did not dare presume to tie them for him. If we did, he determinedly undid and retied them himself!

When Melissa began first grade, I decided to take on a part-time job to help supplement our income. We placed the two little boys in daycare for the mornings. The image of Chrissie's mournful face watching me through the gate as I drove away is burned into my memory. I wish I could turn back the clock and do things differently. I had no idea how little time I had left with my son.

Always a healthy child, in January of 1999, when Chrissie was three we noticed that he began getting car sick. We didn't think too much of it since it only happened occasionally, and we usually found a good reason for it, such as eating too much cake at a birthday party or beginning a long trip without eating

> *I wish I could turn back the clock and do things differently. I had no idea how little time I had left with my son.*

breakfast. But then we noticed that he had developed a squint. We went from eye specialist to optometrist to orthoptist, and finally concluded that he had a sixth nerve paresis, which had possibly become damaged in a fall off the bunk bed. We began eye exercises with him and he started wearing an eye patch. Things did not improve, however, and when he began experiencing dizzy spells and falling over, we became alarmed. We took him to the pediatrician, who immediately recommended a CT scan. What they found changed everything.

On February 28, Chrissie was diagnosed with a brain stem glioma, a cancerous tumor located in the very center of his brain. The neuro-surgeon gave us no hope. "There is no effective treatment. Take your son home and give him the best quality of life possible." My first reaction to bad news is always denial and a feeling of numbness. I talked brightly with Chrissie about how we were going to go to the pharmacy and buy him some eye patches with cute little animals on them. Perhaps talking about something else would make the nightmare go away. My husband understood the implications of the news quicker than I did, as he broke down in tears. I looked up at him, shocked to see him crying. As the days passed and the awful reality sank in, we were both utterly devastated.

We faced a dilemma, as right before Chrissie's diagnosis, my husband and I had resigned from our jobs in anticipation of our move to South Korea. We were due to leave at the end of April. We believed that God had led us this far, and that He had a reason for what was happening to Chrissie. We could only trust God and take one day at a time. We both decided to quit our jobs immediately—even though we were supposed to work a month's notice—so that we could take care of Chrissie. My husband's boss kindly gave him an extra month's salary and wonderful family and friends sent us donations, which provided for our needs.

Chrissie was hospitalized shortly after the CT scan, where the doctors put him on an IV to control his vomiting. At this time he also had an MRI scan which confirmed his diagnosis. The tumor sat in the middle of his brain like a squash ball. However, after two days we took Chrissie home with the IV because the hospital frightened him.

Chrissie found the limitations of his illness distressing. One Sabbath I took Melissa and Kyle to Sabbath School, while Chrissie stayed home with my husband. As I strapped his sister and brother into their car seats, Chrissie made his way up to the car to say goodbye. Clutching his "nanum" in one hand, he clung to the half open window where Kyle sat and sadly repeated, "Kylie, Kylie, Kylie." He longed to go with his big brother whom he adored.

Chrissie deteriorated before our eyes: vomiting constantly; so dizzy that he wanted to lie down all the time; losing the use of the left side of his body. Chrissie had always been a strong-willed child, and he determined to remain independent. He insisted on eating, even though he vomited immediately, and when he couldn't walk to the bathroom anymore, he crawled on his hands and knees. Eventually we were forced to put him back in diapers. How humiliating for an independent three-year-old this must have been. He lost his ability to swallow, and finally became unable to speak. One heartbreaking day the doctors told us to stop feeding Chrissie, as his body simply could not digest anything. As a mother, my instinct compelled me to nurture my child and it felt unbelievably cruel to be unable to feed him.

We requested our pastor and the elders of our church to come and hold an anointing service for Chrissie in our home. We had Chrissie in the living room with us when they arrived, but before long, he crawled his way down the passage to the room where his sister and brother slept and climbed into his bed. The pastor went and lay on the bed with Chrissie and prayed and anointed him there. We committed our son into God's hands and truly believed that if He so willed, He would heal him.

However, we couldn't bear to simply do nothing, and tried every avenue possible for Chrissie. We contacted a radiation oncologist at Groote Schuur Hospital in Cape Town. She agreed to see Chrissie. After her examination she decided to try radiation therapy. Chrissie began five weeks of intensive radiation treatment. They made him a special Perspex mask which he wore during treatment. Too sick to move, the claustrophobic mask must have distressed him. But he never complained. The powerful radiation pounded both sides of his head over his ears. In the beginning his condition worsened, and one night we feared we would lose him. The doctor saw him the following morning and considered stopping the treatment because Chrissie didn't seem to be responding. However, she had one more option. "I would like to try hyper-fractionating his treatment. This will mean giving him two shorter bursts a day, instead of one long treatment."

Suddenly we noticed a dramatic improvement! From a catatonic, helpless little boy who couldn't even hold his own head up, Chrissie started to respond. Having eaten nothing for three weeks, he was skin and bones. We began feeding him a special formula with a syringe and he grew a little stronger each day. There came a day when he said his first few words again and our joy knew no bounds! He began to sit up and to eat and speak. Eventually he began walking again. One month after his treatment ended we took him back to the hospital to show the doctors and radiation therapists how well he was doing. We believed a miracle had occurred. But the doctor could give us no guarantees. She warned, "Chrissie could live for two months, or for another five years. He might have learning difficulties, or hearing problems. If the tumor does return, it will be bad, for Chrissie has received the maximum radiation he can ever have. There is nothing more we can do for him." But this did not concern us. Our little boy had returned from the valley of death.

We went home rejoicing, believing that God had healed Chrissie. We refused to let any doubts creep into our minds. Chrissie did remarkably well. He recovered completely, apart from the hair which he lost around his ears from the radiation. We put him on an intensive vitamin program and watched his diet carefully. A little trooper, he swallowed his pills faithfully every day.

We had postponed our departure for South Korea until the end of June. Now we packed up the few clothes and books we were taking with us and sold everything else we owned to start a new life. The parting from my parents at the airport felt bittersweet, for we planned to be away indefinitely. Little did we know that they were holding Chrissie for the last time.

On our way to Seoul we stopped over in Singapore for six days. Enjoying our visit, we did notice that Chrissie wasn't eating well, and often had headaches. We forced ourselves to believe that this was a result of the radiation therapy and that he just needed time to recover from the side effects. However, two days after we arrived in Seoul, Chrissie vomited. Our hearts sank. We desperately wanted to believe that he had a tummy bug, but deep down we knew that the tumor had begun to grow again. He suffered with terrible headaches. The radiation therapy had created scar tissue and the tumor couldn't grow sideways. It grew *up* instead and caused tremendous pressure in Chrissie's brain. When the pain became intolerable, he covered his head completely with his "nanum," and this soothed him somewhat.

In spite of his illness, Chrissie's quirky personality shone through. We shared a precious moment as he cuddled in bed with me early one morning. The strap of my nightgown had slipped off my shoulder. Suddenly I felt Chrissie's little hands gently putting it back in place. My heart welled up with tenderness for him. That was Chrissie—particular about having order in his world. He inherited that from his mother!

As the tumor grew like a weed in Chrissie's brain, we descended into the horror of the nightmare all over again. Chrissie vomited constantly and couldn't keep any food down. He loved strawberry flavored soy milk and begged me to give it to him, but I didn't dare, for it came straight back up. He grew even thinner than he had been before. Lying on his right side, he endured excruciating pain in his head without complaint. This time his speech wasn't affected as badly, and he could still communicate with us. All he wanted was for someone to lie with him. He didn't want to be touched, as it must have been painful for him, but he did want us to be near.

Thankfully, we lived close to an Adventist hospital, and were put in touch with a wonderful doctor who attended one of my husband's English classes. He, together with the hospital oncologist, helped us with Chrissie. They gave us medications and IV equipment so that we were able to care for him at home. Our schedules worked out so that one of us could be with Chrissie all the time. My husband taught in the mornings and evenings, and I taught in the afternoons. The other teachers at the institute were compassionate and caring and gave us much support and love. Somehow we continued to function. But I became so sleep deprived that at times I stood in front of my students while teaching and my mind went completely blank.

As Chrissie grew worse, he withdrew more and more into himself. Eventually, the only person he wanted near him was my husband. When he could not be there, Chrissie would tolerate me, but only until my husband returned. Although I understood that Chrissie could only focus on one person, it felt like a knife in my heart. My husband confessed to me later, "I thought you resented me because Chrissie chose me over you." But I assured him that I never felt that way. I had only admiration for the wonderful manner in which my husband took care of Chrissie, willing him to live with every fiber of his being.

Towards the end of July, we rushed Chrissie to the ICU at the hospital. He burned with constant fevers, as the tumor began to affect the temperature control in his brain. He breathed shallowly and sometimes stopped breathing for a few seconds. This scared us and we felt he should be in the hospital. When the doctors saw him that day they told us that Chrissie didn't have more than a few hours to live. We were devastated.

Once again I felt numb and unable to cry. One of our fellow English teachers came to see us in the ICU and when she saw Chrissie, burst into tears. This startled me. Being with Chrissie every day, I did not notice how emaciated he had become. Soon after arriving in the ICU, Chrissie began having seizures. Fear clutched at my heart as the reality sank in that we were going to lose him.

Chrissie lived for another ten days. The doctors put him on medication while in the hospital, and his condition stabilized. Our doctor friend told us afterwards that if they hadn't put Chrissie on that medication he would have died the same day we brought him in. We were a little upset to find this out because we felt that he had to suffer those extra ten days unnecessarily. We had told the doctors that we didn't want to prolong Chrissie's life. Somehow, with the language barrier, they did not understand us and believed we wanted them to do everything they could for our little boy. Yet, they were all so kind and caring and we were extremely grateful for their help when we felt helpless.

The days Chrissie spent in the hospital were difficult for all of us. Aware of everything, he cried for us if he woke up and we weren't there. But at the same time, Melissa and Kyle, aged eight and five, needed us, too. Too young to fully comprehend the situation, they were scared and confused. One night I stayed in the hospital with Chrissie, dozing off and on as I tried to get comfortable at the foot of his bed. Early the following morning, while Melissa and Kyle were still sleeping, my husband came with a friend's scooter to pick me up. We had no one to stay with the children, but he hoped to be back before they woke up. However, as he left, the heavens opened in one of Korea's noisy early morning summer thunderstorms. Kyle hated thunderstorms and always called for me at the first clap of thunder. This time I was not there. My husband and I arrived home to find our front door standing wide open and the children missing! We were frantic. My husband rode around the neighborhood looking for them and I called everyone I knew. Finally we decided to call the police. Suddenly our Korean neighbors, whom we had never met, appeared at our door with Melissa and Kyle in tow. In their limited English they explained that they heard the children screaming out on our front steps and took them home to comfort them until we returned. Weak with relief, I felt devastated at the way our lives seemed to be unravelling.

After a few days we took Chrissie out of the hospital, as it became too exhausting to keep him there. In Korea, parents are expected to take care of the patient full-time. The nurses' job is strictly to administer medication. We couldn't handle taking care of Chrissie full-time at the hospital, so we set up the IV once more at home and attended to him there. It tore us apart to watch him suffer. He screamed every time the doctor changed his IV needle. On one occasion, in the middle of this procedure, Chrissie sobbed, "Daddy, please pray to Jesus for me!" My husband administered morphine to him through the IV. One day, while waiting for his dose of morphine, Chrissie was in agony. "Mommy, I'm so desperate!" My heart broke.

During the last few days of his life Chrissie stopped speaking. However, we knew he was aware of us, because when we spoke to him he sighed or moved his arm. Eventually, all he could move was his right arm. One evening, Melissa and Kyle played in the living room with a train set that a friend had given them. When I went into the bedroom to check on Chrissie, silent tears were running down his cheeks. How he must have longed to be with his brother and sister, yet he could not express himself.

The hours of darkness were the worst. One night Chrissie suffered seizures for three hours. We lay with him and held him. Another night he fought to breathe and we expected every breath to be his last. We were exhausted. Finally, on the night of August 8, we saw his breathing become more labored. He had an infection and choked on mucous constantly because of his inability to swallow. We suctioned the mucous from his throat with a syringe.

By the morning of August 9, as he grew weaker, his breathing became extremely shallow. His body felt cold to the touch and his heartbeat grew faint. My husband went to teach that morning, but when I felt Chrissie's face finally growing cold and his heartbeat almost undetectable, I called him back home. Shortly before 9:00 a.m., in those few moments when I left the room to make the call, Chrissie took his last breath. I regret to this day that I missed holding my son as he fell asleep in death. At the age of four years and three months, our little boy was gone.

Our new friends rallied around us, offering their support. However, I felt frustrated that I had to sit and talk to people in the living room, when all I wanted was to be in the bedroom saying goodbye to my son. We held the funeral the following day, and buried Chrissie in a beautiful Adventist cemetery about an hour from Seoul. His grave is unmarked, but I know that God marked his resting place, and one day soon He will raise Chrissie to life—perfect, beautiful, and pain-free. Heaven is infinitely precious to me and I long for the day when an angel will place Chrissie in my arms.

As I packed up Chrissie's tiny shirts and shorts to send to my sister for her boys, I set aside some of his favorite belongings to keep close to my heart forever. As I write, I touch each memory: one of his precious "nanums" that he could never be without; a pastel colored crocheted blanket that my mom made for him when he was born; his miniature green and yellow racing car toothbrush; his blue sunhat and a pair of purple sunglasses just his size; a toddler board book called "Mary's Good Deed;" and a tiny plastic "Hercules" action figure. Time heals our wounds but can never erase our memories.

In the many e-mails from friends all around the world we saw how God used Chrissie's life to touch many hearts and draw them closer to Him. It hurts that Chrissie had to suffer so much, but I know God had a special purpose for my strong and brave little boy.

Chapter 4

Surrender

"Say a quiet yes to God and he'll be there in no time."

(James 4:8, MSG)

After Chrissie's death I spiraled into a place of darkness. I had no idea how to process what had happened to my son. In my human reasoning, I needed to understand why, and as a parent, I blamed myself for the suffering of my child. I endured a period of extreme remorse and soul-searching with God, for I believed that I caused the death of my son. I did not follow the best of diets while pregnant with Chrissie. Now the thought tormented me, "Maybe the tumor began to form in his tiny brain as he grew in my womb?" One night, a few days after the funeral, I sobbed out this tale of woe in the arms of my husband. Illogical reasoning perhaps, but it tortured my soul until I laid my burden on God and found peace. This was the first and only time I cried after we lost Chrissie. My feelings and emotions remained trapped deep inside of me, unable to find their way out.

My husband and I were locked in our separate worlds of grieving, incapable of comforting each other. I wanted to talk about Chrissie, to somehow keep him a part of our lives, but my husband found this too painful. I felt guilty speaking to others about Chrissie in front of him, as it upset him. He found comfort in the company of his students. Since many of these students were young women, this brought all my insecurities to the surface. I did not have time to deal with the knowledge of my husband's affair before Chrissie got sick. Now the agony of his betrayal hit me with full force again.

Newly arrived in a foreign country, we had no family support. The people that we worked with were kind to us, but we hardly knew them and couldn't open our grieving hearts to them. For six months I lived in a black hole from which I seemed unable to escape. Food became a poor comforter. I gained weight and my health deteriorated. After a bad bout of flu I developed symptoms of chronic fatigue and fibromyalgia. Exhausted, and struggling to keep up with my teaching job, I had strange aches and pains all over my body. I knew I needed to do something before I developed a serious illness.

I began putting into practice the health principles that I heard about in church all my life. These principles included: good nutrition, exercise, drinking water, sunshine, temperance (avoiding that which is harmful and using wisely that which is healthy), fresh air, rest, and trust in Divine power. I took my eating habits in hand, watching my portions and avoiding junk foods. The extra weight began to melt away. I took daily walks up and down the small mountain behind our apartment and immediately felt better about myself. My energy returned, and the aches and pains disappeared. As my body healed, my mind began to clear. I became more spiritually aware.

The experience I had with God just before Chrissie got sick had been lost to a large degree as I churned in the turmoil of my troubled marriage, Chrissie's illness, our move to Korea, and then Chrissie's death. But God called to my heart, "Turn to Me. Let Me be your source of comfort and strength." He reminded me of the peace He gave me as I prayed for Chrissie, a short while before he died, entrusting my son into His hands and surrendering to whatever He deemed best. I don't remember feeling angry or bitter toward God. Despite my tremendous pain, I believed Him to be in control.

During this time of spiritual awakening, we attended a weekend retreat for all the English teachers, with a guest speaker from the United States. He represented a ministry called "FAST" and shared with us a wonderful method of Scripture memorization. Inspired, I drank in everything he taught, implementing it in my life immediately. His method included regular review to keep the Scriptures in your long-term memory. I continue to use his method to this day, and the verses I memorized way back then are still in my memory bank. This retreat became a turning point in my life, and the beginning of my true conversion. There is power in God's Word! He began transforming me as I hid His Word in my heart.

This retreat became a turning point in my life, and the beginning of my true conversion. There is power in God's Word! He began transforming me as I hid His Word in my heart.

One day I found a Biblical-based book on fasting at the Salvation Army bookstore in Seoul. The idea intrigued me. I tried fasting once before, but the hunger pangs overcame me and I never made it past lunchtime! This time I managed to fast for three days and felt an amazing sense of accomplishment. The fruit of self-denial is self-control. I began to learn how to control my appetite and moved to eating two meals a day. When I discovered the newly-arisen raw food movement on the internet, it sparked my interest. I tend to be an all-or-nothing person, and this seemed like the perfect way to eat. I decided to work towards achieving a 100% raw, plant-based diet. The more I practiced regular fasting (fasting twenty-four hours each week), and the more raw foods I incorporated into my diet, the better I felt. Even Melissa and Kyle enthused, "Mom, you're a much nicer person when you're eating raw!"

The more my mind cleared, the more I grew spiritually as I responded to the impressions of the Holy Spirit. I finally surrendered my heart completely to Christ and chose to let go of everything that separated me from Him. This happened during a vacation in South Africa with my children in September of 2001. My sister, Jenny, and brother-in-law, Richard, welcomed us into their home, and by their wonderful example inspired me to make that surrender.

I longed to have an intimate relationship with Christ. My struggling marriage magnified the emptiness in my heart. On this particular vacation, I knew the time had come for me to get rid of the cherished idols in my life. The books I read, the music I listened to, and the movies I watched, had to go. I wrestled with God for days, but I knew that I had to give them up, for they took His place in my heart. I cried bitterly after giving away the music CDs that had been my comfort during the months after losing Chrissie. What a struggle, but what joy when I finally surrendered and told God, "I want You more than I want these idols—these substitutes for what only You can give me." I wanted Him to live in my heart without rival. I have never regretted that decision for a moment. I still had a long way to go, but from that moment on, God began working with power in my life, molding me into the woman He wanted me to be.

It thrilled my heart to see how the Lord worked to give me victory over many things that had bothered my conscience for a long time. The beautiful thing for me was that I didn't have to grit my teeth and say, "I'm not going to do this," but He took away the desire, so that I didn't even want to do those things anymore. It was never my intention to try and force my husband to change. In my enthusiasm for what the Lord had done in my life, I may have handled things badly upon my return to Korea. Since communication between my husband and I had deteriorated considerably by this time, he did not understand why I suddenly made all these changes. I tried to leave him to be free to choose how he wanted to live his life, but perhaps there were times when he perceived me to be judging him and disapproving of him, when that was not my intention. How much I now regret that we never talked these things through.

I spent ten years in Asia—most of that time in South Korea, with nine months working in Thailand, and a year back in South Africa sandwiched in-between. I stayed interested in the raw food diet, even eating 100% raw for four months straight. I lost weight, felt amazing, and believed that my struggles with my weight and emotional eating were over. I began studying for a degree in natural health by correspondence. However, as the months and years passed, I felt my husband and I growing further and further apart. I tried everything I could to remedy the problem, but seemed powerless to change the situation.

In 2005, work circumstances separated the children and me from my husband for one year. However, just a few days after our little family reunited, my world shattered all over again. I discovered that for four years my husband had been having an affair. Once again I forgave him instantly, but I did not know how to pick up the pieces of my broken heart. My husband assured me that he had ended the affair and wanted to save our marriage. Yet he did nothing to rebuild my trust in him. I tried everything I could to show him that I loved him. But every night I went to bed alone, feeling rejected and unloved. Despite my best efforts, my marriage deteriorated rapidly, and as it did, so did my eating habits. I swung from one extreme to the other—eating healthy and then bingeing. Eventually my self-loathing became so strong, that on one or two occasions I made myself throw up after bingeing. I had reached a breaking point and knew that I needed to take action before I lost my health and my sanity.

Chapter 5

Wilderness Journey

"The Lord is close to those whose hearts are breaking."

(Psalm 34:18)

There are many wilderness areas in South Africa, truly wildly remote and beautiful. But the wilderness I experienced had nothing to do with the wild and beautiful country that became my refuge. The problems confronting my husband and I seemed insurmountable after the death of our son. After experiencing such a traumatic event in a relationship, many marriages don't make it. The broken trust between us compounded the issue. Failing health reflected my shattered heart. I decided to initiate a separation—an agonizing decision for me, but one I felt I had to make. I had no desire for a divorce but knew that I needed to put some distance between us. Beyond that, I had no answers.

Richard and Jenny live on a beautiful farm named Island View. On a clear day you can see all the way to the ocean. I asked them if Kyle and I could come and stay for a while. I will be eternally grateful to them for allowing us to come for such an extended period—which became four years—as well as to my parents for opening their home on the farm to us. It became a sanctuary for me, a time of healing and growing.

Soon after the separation, a friend of my mom wrote to her, "This morning I came to your name in my journal but for some strange reason the Lord had me pray for Alison—that she would arise and be called blessed. He has a beautiful plan for her and is very close to her. She has gone through a lot more pain than many of us are aware but it is in that pain that God does amazing things for her and for many others." Little did any of us know the path I still had to walk, and the amazing things that God would yet do!

I had the opportunity for a precious time of bonding with my son as I homeschooled him—or he homeschooled himself, with the math help of my dad—for his final two years of school. I also finished studying the natural health degree which I had begun working on in South Korea.

Melissa worked as an editorial intern at Young Disciple Ministries in the United States and needed to return to South Africa for visa purposes. She joined us on the farm and her stay turned into a year as she waited for her visa to be processed. We became roommates, and enjoyed a special time of bonding, too, as we all dealt with the breakup of our family. Richard and Jenny spent countless hours counseling Melissa, Kyle, and I through this difficult time. Their love and support and wise counsel blessed us beyond measure. Jenny is four years younger than me, and yet she seemed to be the "older sister" as I floundered in the chaos of my life.

This oasis in time allowed me to heal emotionally from the loss of my son and a stressful marriage. Quiet and peaceful on the farm, I heard God's still small voice speaking to my soul. I spent much time in prayer and Bible study, soaking up God's Word. I took walks on the dusty farm roads with my sister, enjoying the expansive blue sky, green fields, delicate wild flowers, and heart-to-heart talks. One sunny afternoon, with an aching heart, I took a walk alone and cried out to God, "My pain feels overwhelming today. Won't You please come and comfort me with Your presence? I want to know that You are near." At that very moment a cool breeze sprang up and caressed my bare arms. I felt loved from the top of my head to the soles of my feet.

I believe this tranquil period of healing, learning and growing spiritually prepared me for the next fiery trial in my life. Psalms 73:25 and 26 became filled with meaning for me: "Whom have I in heaven but you? And I desire no one on earth as much as you! My health fails; my spirits droop, yet God remains! He is the strength of my heart; he is mine forever!" As I brought my brokenness to God He became my Heavenly Husband.

2 Corinthians 5:17 says, "When someone becomes a Christian, he becomes a brand-new person inside. He is not the same anymore. A new life has begun!" As I allowed the Holy Spirit to work in my heart, as I let go of trying to find the strength in myself, He began to change my think-

ing—I started seeing how my old ways of eating were losing their hold on me. At this time I came across a book called *Get Thin, Stay Thin* by Arthur and Judy Halliday. They wrote about what they called "disordered eating"—eating that is out of control, out of God's order. In one exercise they suggested I describe my disordered eating. I wrote:

> I am preoccupied with food and eating—thinking too much about when I'm going to eat, what I'm going to eat, how much I'm going to eat, thinking about recipes and favorite foods, etc. I use food to try to numb my emotional pain and satisfy my unfulfilled yearnings for intimacy. When I feel bad I have a compulsion to eat in an unhealthy way: to eat too much or to eat things that are not good for me. I have lost the joy and pleasure in eating because my lack of control makes me afraid of getting fat or harming my body, leading to some serious disease. Food is a compulsion, an obsession, and an idol—at times completely taking over my mind, controlling me and affecting every area of my life. This obsession and its resultant behavior (overeating, especially) separates me from my God and takes away my desire for prayer and Bible study. It makes my mind foggy and unable to hear the Holy Spirit. It saps my energy, taking away my desire and ability to exercise the way I should, and makes me a grumpy, unpleasant person to be around. Food has become an enemy that I fear and feel enslaved by.

I saw myself as flawed, unwanted, unlovable, and trapped in my comfort eating habits. But God wanted to help me understand that He saw me as a precious daughter made in His image, and infinitely loved by Him. He accepted me as I was. He wanted to set me free. As the Holy Spirit changed my thinking, I saw how He got to the root of my disordered eating—showing me things from the past that made me the person I had become. He helped me to acknowledge my pain, forgive, and be released from bondage. He taught me how to let go of all my rules and regulations (my desperate attempts to control my eating) and to be free to trust Him with my eating, my weight, and my life.

I decided to commit to a ten-day fast, seeking the Lord earnestly for help in the following, specific areas: appetite, my marriage and future, my children. I prayed that my Heavenly Husband would do something supernatural in me, for I could not deal with myself. I had never fasted this long before and found it extremely difficult. I struggled with terrible nausea from day two on, but by God's grace I completed it. During the fast

I saw the Lord working in the lives of my children. Melissa had an amazing change in attitude and learned to be positive and content in a difficult situation, and Kyle went on a life-changing mission trip to Zimbabwe. I praised God for answered prayers.

After a year, both my children left for work and school in the United States. My heart ached, as I had never been without either of them before. It felt strange not to be in a mother's role anymore. At the end of 2012, Melissa brought a special young man, Daniel, to the farm to visit for a month. We all grew to love him. They were later engaged to be married in Canada. My niece and I happily planned our trip to Canada for the wedding.

As the date for our departure grew closer, I reflected on four ways in which God speaks to us: through Scripture; through impressions of the Holy Spirit; through our own common sense; and through providential circumstances. I learned that where these four harmonize, it is safe to say that God is speaking. I felt a strong impression from my Heavenly Husband telling me to get my affairs in order, to prepare for the possibility that I would stay in Canada. There seemed to be harmony in what I heard from Him. He spoke to me through two verses of Scripture. Ezekiel 12:3 said, "Pack whatever you can carry on your back and leave your home— go somewhere else." In Habakkuk 1:5, He said to me, "Look, and be amazed! You will be astounded at what I am about to do! For I am going to do something in your own lifetime that you will have to see to believe." My own common sense and the providential opportunity to make this trip to Canada for the wedding further confirmed my impression. Excited to see what the Lord would do in my life, I praised Him for this chance to be with my children.

Shortly before we left for the wedding in Canada, my husband finally decided he wanted a divorce. My heart ached, for I didn't want it to end this way. But at the same time I felt a sense of relief that the uncertainty of the three-and-a-half-year separation had come to an end. The divorce proceedings began with a South African lawyer, a time-consuming process as paperwork had to be sent back and forth between South Africa and South Korea, where my husband still lived. I left for Canada knowing that a court appearance would be necessary whenever I returned, to finalize the divorce.

In Canada, Daniel's family welcomed us warmly, and we all had a wonderful time preparing for the wedding. Kyle came from California, and at the last minute, Jenny, Richard, and their two boys joined us from

South Africa. Melissa and Daniel were married on August 12, 2013, in a beautiful outdoor ceremony.

I longed to stay in Canada, near my daughter. While there for the wedding, I went on a job interview for a girl's dean position at a local Seventh-day Adventist boarding academy, just a short way from where Melissa and Daniel would be living. The school seemed interested in me and requested that I come through their one-week orientation program. However, during that week I became more and more convinced that the job was not for me. I found this agonizing, because I desperately wanted to stay in Canada. I felt a complete failure and thought that my fears had gotten the best of me. Looking back, I see now that the strong impression I had was more than just my fears and insecurities—I believe the Holy Spirit put a check on my spirit, for He knew this would not be the best situation for me. God knew what lay ahead. He wanted me to be where He had prepared everything necessary to get me through the fiery trial that loomed in the not-so-distant future.

> *God knew what lay ahead. He wanted me to be where He had prepared everything necessary to get me through the fiery trial that loomed in the not-so-distant future.*

I returned to South Africa, disappointed that I seemed to have misinterpreted God's voice before leaving for Canada. On October 3, 2013, I presented myself at the courthouse and the divorce became final. My marriage of almost twenty-seven years ended, and a new chapter in my life began.

Chapter 6
Wildwood

**"Throw yourselves wholeheartedly and full-time ...
into God's way of doing things."**
(Romans 6:13, MSG)

When the job in Canada did not work out, I had no idea what to do with my life. During a conversation with Melissa one day, she suggested, "What about Wildwood?" I had forgotten about it. Wildwood Lifestyle Center is a natural health care center set back in the hills of North West Georgia, near Chattanooga, Tennessee. There are acres of trails to walk, amid the beauty and peace of nature. It is a facility where people can come to reverse many of the illnesses prevalent in today's society. Wildwood is known for combining the medicine of nature with modern medicine, and works hard to benefit the mind, body, and spirit. They believe in healing through changing lives, and not just treating symptoms.

Health problems are tackled with a healthy diet, exercise, herbs and supplements, massage, and hydrotherapy of various kinds. There are cooking classes to help people get started, walks out in the sunshine, and early to bed and early to rise times! Lectures are presented on the eight laws of health, as well as a variety of interesting health topics. Wildwood also runs a Center for Health Evangelism, where students of all ages come from countries around the world to be trained as medical missionaries.

The courses offered include: Applied Physiology, Hydrotherapy, Massage, Nutrition and Vegetarian Cooking, Basic Gardening, Herbs, Mission Medicine and First Aid, Mental Health, Disease and Treatment, as well as a number of Biblical and practical Christian living subjects.

I had known about Wildwood for a long time, since a few of my mom's friends went to do the medical missionary training many years ago. A number of my own friends from college days were currently working there. With my interest in natural health, Melissa's suggestion grabbed my attention. I immediately applied to Wildwood, and then waited (impatiently) for an answer. Already October, I hoped to be accepted in time for the spring training session, which began the following January.

One month later I received an answer from Wildwood. I had been accepted as a work scholarship student to do the medical missionary training course starting in the middle of January. My Wildwood tuition deposit, visa costs, and plane ticket cost me everything I owned, but I finally had a sense of purpose.

Excited to be leaving, I felt torn saying goodbye to my parents and Jenny and Richard and their children. I didn't know when I would see them again. As we enjoyed a farewell meal together, my dad gave one of his rare speeches:

> We have gathered as Island View family to celebrate the launching of a new chapter in the life of Alison. As her parents, she has been part of our lives since before she was born. To her siblings she has been part of their lives since they were born. We are happy the previous chapter of your life can now be closed, and that you can look forward to a new environment, new people, new challenges, and new opportunities. We believe the Lord has led you this far and He will continue to lead you into the future. Rest assured that as long as we have a home it will be yours as well. We believe you have enjoyed Divine protection this far—in spite of falling off the kitchen table and damaging your neck, falling off a motorbike and damaging your knee, and surviving when the car you were travelling in collided with a cow. Who knows how many other close shaves there were of which we may not be aware? I believe that everything that has happened to us in the past is a preparation for our future in God's plan of things. There will be an empty space at our table, an empty room in our home. The sound of your touch at the piano will be sorely missed. We are sad, but happy for you, and wish you God's richest blessings as you step out into the future.

Know that God is there before you, and He will never leave you nor forsake you.

A few days later I stepped out of my parents' nest for the second time. It took all the courage I could muster to embark on this new adventure alone, but my Heavenly Father gave me this promise, "Be strong! Be courageous! Do not be afraid of them! For the Lord your God will be with you. He will neither fail you nor forsake you" (Deuteronomy 31:6).

I trusted that He would be with me every step of the way. The long journey appeared daunting, as I had never flown alone before. I flew to Johannesburg, spent twelve hours in the airport, and then endured a seventeen-hour direct flight to Atlanta. After a two-hour shuttle drive to Chattanooga, one of the Wildwood staff met me and drove me to Wildwood. Arriving in the middle of winter, everything looked drab and brown. However, the size of the campus and the many trees impressed me. I felt like pinching myself. "Am I really here?" My dreams were coming true.

As a student, I moved into the girl's dorm and had a roommate. I found this amusing. It reminded me of my college days and I felt like a teenager again. I chose to embrace it and enjoyed the experience. However, although all the girls in the dorm were sweet, being one of the oldest students, I felt extremely lonely at times. I missed my family, especially my children, and the sense of belonging I had with them. Kyle began college in South Africa (we virtually crossed paths in the air), and Melissa could not leave Canada until her permanent residence paperwork had been approved. I could not afford to travel and had no prospect of seeing my children any time soon.

My friend Colleen proved to be a wonderful support to me at this time. Leaving home and adopting a new country can be intimidating and scary. It's especially wonderful when you meet people from your home country. There is an instant camaraderie and understanding. I felt that way meeting up with Colleen again at Wildwood. We studied at the same college in South Africa many years before. Colleen and my sister, Caroline, were friends, but she and I never connected at that time. Our lives went in different directions when we left college.

After having no contact for many years, one day in 2007, while living in Korea, I received a Facebook message from Colleen. She asked me for my sister's e-mail address. Colleen and I began an e-mail and Facebook conversation, sharing our common challenges with eating and our experiments with the raw food diet. Colleen sent me the link to her blog. As I read her posts about her walk with the Lord, I felt impressed by this woman of God. I confided, "I sense in you a kindred spirit! Although, after briefly browsing through your blog I believe you are further along the narrow way than I am!" As Colleen shared more with me about her walk with God and her struggles, and how often she poured out her heart to God, I became increasingly inspired by her.

I admitted to Colleen in the midst of my marriage troubles, "Your words of encouragement and your prayers mean so much to me. Some days I feel like such a mess!" She encouraged me, "Thanks for sharing your journey. I love your heart for the Lord!" Appreciating her friendship through this difficult period, little did I realize what an important role Colleen would play in my life in the future.

From the moment I arrived at Wildwood, Colleen and her husband, Trevor, took me under their wing and became like family to me as I struggled to adjust to being alone and in a new country and situation. They willingly drove me wherever I needed to go and made sure to invite me for Sabbath lunch with them every week, unless they were away. Colleen and I picked up our friendship as though we had always known each other, and I found it comforting to have a "sister" in which to confide.

Trevor served as Administrator of the Lifestyle Center and Clinic, and Colleen as the Guest Services Manager. They became my bosses! Being part of the work scholarship program, I attended one class in the morning, and then worked at my assigned job in the Guest Services office the rest of the day. My work as "alumni coordinator" required me to keep in touch with the lifestyle guests after their stay, in order to encourage them in their new lifestyle. The job involved a great deal of phone work, which I found a huge challenge. I hate talking on the telephone! Another of my duties involved becoming acquainted with the guests while they were on the lifestyle program—so that I could connect with them on the phone later. This presented another challenge, as I have always been a shy person and find meeting new people stressful.

However, I tried to give it my best shot, as I believed that God had brought me to Wildwood and placed me in this specific position. I worked in the same office as Colleen, and her leadership blessed me. I appreciated her patience with me as I learned a new job. Her gentle and compassionate way with people on the phone, and her prayers with them, inspired me. She had a heart for people and always gave of herself to others.

Weariness overwhelmed me in my first days at Wildwood. The two noisy trains that ran on either side of the campus and came by at frequent intervals disturbed my sleep. The days were long and I had a delayed reaction to the stress of the whole move. I sat in class, worship, or church, thinking, "What am I doing here? I don't fit in!" I had a hard time seeing God's purpose for my life. Aware of my inadequacy, I knew I needed to surrender my heart and let God grow me and use me as He saw fit.

As the weeks passed, my tiredness increased. It didn't feel like ordinary tiredness—more like the chronic fatigue that I had experienced before. I knew I needed to do something about it. I tried eating more raw foods, and taking vitamins and herbs, but nothing seemed to help. I had frequent migraine headaches and ached all over.

In my loneliness and exhaustion, I reached out to the God who had always been faithful to me. I felt the reassurance of His hand over my life and His sweet presence with me. I became aware of how He loved me through my friends at Wildwood, and I longed for Him to love others through me. What a privilege to be His heart and hands to bless others! As my first spring at Wildwood arrived, I enjoyed the beauty all around me and felt new life bursting in my heart. "Thank you, Lord, for the gift of this new beginning at Wildwood."

I learned more and more in my classes each week. In one class we heard that Wildwood has a 63% success rate in treating cancer, compared to traditional medicine's 3%. Our teacher challenged us: "What a difference it could make if we had more lifestyle centers treating cancer in this way! If we believed and trusted in the healthy ways God desires us to live, we could be the object lesson of health and prosperity to the world—just as the ancient Israelites were meant to be. Too often we simply don't believe what God says!"

After three months at Wildwood, I continued to dread the phone work. I learned in another of my classes that God wants to use our natural aptitudes (what we're good at) and our passions (what we like doing) to give the good news of Him to the world. I became convinced that telephone work was *not* a natural aptitude or passion of mine! I felt desperate.

The question went around and around in my mind: "Does God want me to continue doing this job in order to test and strengthen my character? Or is He testing me to see if I will have the courage to go to those in authority over me and tell them I don't want to do this anymore, instead of meekly complying and being miserable?" I felt pressured because I didn't want to let Trevor and Colleen down. I also felt pressured because no one understood my aversion to the phone and thought I simply needed to overcome my fears. But I wanted to have a job that I could do well, and at the same time be passionate about. I didn't know the answer to this dilemma. When I eventually plucked up the courage to share my struggle with the phone work, Colleen listened sympathetically.

Chapter 7
Part of the Team

"The trials of life are God's workmen, to remove the impurities and roughness from our characters."

(Ellen White, Messages to Young People, p. 117)

Trevor and Colleen discussed my problem, doing their best to understand my position. They decided to find me another place to work. Trevor offered me the option of working in the hydrotherapy department.

Hydrotherapy is the use of water in its three forms—liquid, steam, or ice—to assist the healing process in a number of diseases and health conditions. The Wildwood hydrotherapy department has the capability to administer a variety of treatments, including whirlpool baths, Russian steam bath and sauna, hot blanket and wet sheet packs, pressure contrast showers, salt glow, ice massage, and hot fomentations for different areas of the body. Depending on the patient's condition, treatments may take anywhere from twenty minutes up to two hours or more. Relaxing massages follow the treatments on certain days.

Hydrotherapy and massage were two areas lacking in my health education, and I felt this would be a good opportunity for practical training. Besides, the idea of working one-on-one with the guests in the hydrotherapy department appealed to my introvert personality. I agreed to the change that Trevor suggested: work most of the time in hydro, but continue to assist Colleen in the Guest Services office for a few hours a day with registration paperwork and marketing. Although excited to be working in hydro, I found it stressful trying to learn everything on the job. The girl I shadowed patiently helped me through the learning curve, but I felt extremely awkward.

One Sabbath, while having lunch with Colleen and Trevor, we discussed my visa situation. Trevor suggested, "Why don't you apply to be a full-time worker at Wildwood? Your missionary visa is only valid for six months. If you become a worker, you can obtain a religious work visa, which will give you two-and-a-half years. You can feel more settled and start working towards obtaining permanent residence." I liked the idea and decided to submit my request and let the Lord decide for me. He knew whether He wanted me to be a student or a worker and I was willing to go either way. I sent an e-mail to the Personnel Committee, requesting a position as a worker at Wildwood. Two days later I received the news that I had been accepted as a worker/trainee in the hydrotherapy department. Excited, I thanked God for the wonderful way He took care of me.

There were conditions to my employment. My health degree had not been issued from a Seventh-day Adventist institution, which Wildwood required. So I needed to complete the principle classes (which I attended in the mornings), as well as the hydrotherapy and massage courses, along with physiology, through the Wildwood Online School. I began studying diligently.

However, my visa situation worried me. My current visa expired soon, and I could not apply for the religious work visa until I had completed the required online courses. I studied hard but struggled to find enough time to fit everything into my days. No longer a student, I had to move out of the dorm by the end of June. I lost count of the number of times I had moved in my life, but the upheaval of it all still unsettled me.

A room became available in a house called "Tree-Top" where a number of single ladies resided. Colleen and Trevor helped me move and took me shopping to buy the things I needed to make my room comfortable. Although an old house, I grew to love my room with its wooden floor and big window that looked out into the tops of the trees. It felt like living in a tree house. I continued to eat my lunches in the student cafeteria, but bought a blender and enjoyed making my own green smoothies for breakfast. I had missed them.

Speedily completing the online courses, Wildwood issued my hydrotherapy and massage certificates and applied for a religious work visa just before my current visa expired. As I walked back to the spa to clean up after a treatment one day, Colleen met me. "Have you heard the news?" She beamed at me. "Your visa was approved!" I couldn't believe the answer had come so soon—only five days after the application had been received! This meant that I could stay in the United States—and at Wildwood—and after two years I had the option to apply for permanent residence. I could now go and obtain a social security number and my driver's license. What a sense of relief to know that I would be staying for a while. Colleen and Trevor took me out for lunch to celebrate!

I continued to find my training in hydro extremely challenging. One night I felt discouraged about my lack of skill—particularly in massage. I kept reminding myself that "God doesn't call the qualified—He qualifies the called!" I depended on Him for strength and wisdom and confidence. That week I helped treat an elderly lady coming off smoking cigarettes. We put her in the Russian steam bath every day, and I gave her my first solo back massage! I tried hard to remember all the techniques I had been shown, and fumbled my way through it. Being the first massage of her life, she enthused, "That felt wonderful!" I breathed a sigh of relief. A co-worker instructed me, "Do whatever you do with confidence. The treatments can seem a little scary for someone who has never had hydrotherapy before. Your confidence will go a long way in reassuring them." That advice has served me well!

> *One night I felt discouraged about my lack of skill—particularly in massage. I kept reminding myself that "God doesn't call the qualified—He qualifies the called!"*

I continued suffering with migraine headaches. I thought perhaps all the stress made my neck and shoulder muscles tense. Another aspect of my health began to worry me. Soon after I arrived at Wildwood a recurring problem of eczema on my hand flared up. This had begun many years previously in South Korea, with a sensitivity to dish soap. I tried every natural remedy I could think of, but the condition worsened as the months passed. When I began working in hydro, this was not acceptable when giving massages. In desperation I started using a cortisone cream on it. After a few days I experienced bad lower back pain. I figured it had to be my kidneys, since I noticed a little blood in my urine. In a few days I felt terrible and my supervisor sent me for a thirty-minute sunbath at the spa, then home to rest. I slept for five hours!

I decided to stop using the cortisone cream. I knew I needed to heal the eczema from the inside—manage stress better, build my immune system—but in the meantime I needed a quick fix because it affected my work. Colleen discovered a protocol on the internet for another natural remedy. I decided to give it a try. Taking it for two months, I felt like I had constant morning sickness! But the eczema miraculously began to clear up, until it had completely disappeared! However, this problem was just the tip of the iceberg—a symptom of the global and aggressive attack happening inside my body.

I breathed a sigh of relief when the fall weather arrived. The air felt delightfully cool as I walked outside. My concern had grown over the past months, as I noticed that my legs were like lead and didn't want to go up the hills. I thought the heat and humidity drained my energy, and blamed it on that. I felt weighed down with feelings of chronic fatigue. Insomnia became a regular occurrence. When I tried to sleep, my heart raced and I had a "restless legs" feeling all over my body. At times I felt a prickling/itching sensation under my skin. I couldn't understand why I had these symptoms. I'd heard that Wildwood's location, on the border of Tennessee and Georgia, was a high allergy area. I had also heard that there were many cell phone towers around Chattanooga. I wondered if those things were causing my problems.

A bit skeptical, I decided to Google "cell phone towers," and found that there were literally hundreds of cell phone towers around the Chattanooga area, with twenty towers and one hundred and eighty-six antennae within a four-mile radius of Wildwood. We also had a power line right outside our home at Tree-Top. I found a few articles that spoke about electro-magnetic radiation from cell phone towers and power lines. The symptoms they cause can range from cancer and heart problems to insomnia and skin rashes or prickling/burning skin. I thought that perhaps my lack of energy and insomnia were not just in my head after all!

My menstrual cycle became irregular and I experienced painful cramps that seemed to be getting worse as time passed. I knew that my body felt the consequences of the stresses of the past years. Apart from the dreaded anticipation of my driving test, the stress had eased to a large degree and I felt ready to begin healing. But the harder I tried to take care of my body, the worse my symptoms became. I felt as though my body was betraying me.

My own foolishness prevented me from getting checked out sooner. My aversion to doctors kept me hoping everything would be all right if I just took good care of myself. Since a traumatic childhood experience with the dentist I had avoided doctors, hospitals, needles, and anything related! I only ever went to a doctor when absolutely necessary. I have always been extremely healthy and the minor things that might occasionally crop up were easy to take care of with my knowledge of natural remedies. At forty-eight years old, I figured I probably should be having some pre-menopausal symptoms, so irregular periods did not seem too out of the ordinary. I did not realize that as time passed, I became more and more anemic from the irregular bleeding. I prayed, "Lord please show me why I feel so bad and how to get well." There seemed to be no answer, but I didn't feel ill enough to visit a doctor. In hindsight, I am puzzled at how I managed to function, considering how bad things really were.

During this time, I felt inexplicably compelled to watch an informative online documentary series about cancer. The host interviewed doctors who practiced lifestyle medicine and cancer survivors who healed using natural methods. I did not miss a single episode. I learned that most people die from the direct effects of conventional cancer treatments—not from the cancer itself. I also learned that it is impossible to have cancer if you have an intact immune system. And lifestyle—particularly an alkaline, oxygen-rich lifestyle—provides a 90% protection against cancer.

I found it a fascinating series. Every single cancer survivor confirmed, "Cancer doesn't scare me anymore!" I believe God impressed me to watch this series in order to prepare my mind for the challenging and terrifying decision I would soon have to make.

After living in Tree Top for a few months, I decided I would love a place of my own. I had a wonderful housemate, but as an introvert, felt a need for my own personal space where I could recharge my emotional batteries after work. I requested a change and thankfully something became available. I moved into an apartment behind the Lifestyle Center just before Christmas. I loved the convenience of it, as I literally only had to take about ten steps to be at work. Tiny, but with everything I needed, I thought it just perfect. I couldn't believe I actually had my own little place—for the first time, ever!

Not long after I celebrated the one-year anniversary of my arrival at Wildwood, I seemed to have picked up another health issue. I developed a pain in my chest that started in the front, under my right ribcage. I thought perhaps it was my gallbladder. But then it moved around to the back. I could only sleep on one side at night, and couldn't exercise, because it hurt to breathe deeply. I had no idea what caused this. I did have a bad case of the flu right after I moved into my apartment, but thought the paint fumes might have triggered it. As mysteriously as the pain arrived, it disappeared again, and I never did get around to seeing a doctor.

My confidence in hydro grew. One day, students from the health school across the way came in for a hydro class. The teacher asked me to demonstrate the Russian steam bath. It struck me that only a few months prior I had been scared to death of not being able to do the treatments right. Now here I was, teaching others! God had truly been my teacher.

That week I also had the privilege of giving treatments to a special lady. A medical doctor, she joined the clinic staff at Wildwood, and went through a lifestyle program as a professional observer. I felt honored to work with Dr. N, a beautiful and dedicated physician. As I gave her a particular hydro treatment to help relieve pain, I had no idea how important this young woman would become to me.

God knew what lay ahead and moved everything into place before the storm broke. Around this time, Ed[1] came into my life. I had been at Wildwood for a few months when a friend encouraged me to try a Christian online dating service. After being separated for four years and now divorced, I felt lonely. I had never been on my own, as I married young. Now, for the first time I had to face life alone and I didn't like it very much. I missed belonging to someone and sharing life's experiences together. Even though, after my failed marriage I had somewhat lost faith in the male species, something inside me still hoped that God would give me a second chance.

Extremely skeptical about online dating, I decided to give it a try. However, after a couple of bad experiences, I abandoned the idea. One man had a fake identity, and another man who contacted me ended up being a total mess! I told God, "I'm going to stay off these sites and trust You to bring the right person to me." I lived in the middle of nowhere, which made it difficult to meet someone!

However, about a year later, in March of 2015, I noticed an ad for a Seventh-day Adventist online dating service. Curious, as I hadn't been on this site before, I thought I'd take a look. The site impressed me! But I could not browse without putting up a profile. Feeling a little miffed, I put up a brief profile and told God, "I absolutely refuse to pay any money on this site unless someone messages me and I want to read it."

That night I received an e-mail—from a woman, no less! Curious to see what she wanted, I prayed about it, and decided to pay the subscription fee for one month. Turns out this woman had some questions about Wildwood. I answered them—and never heard from her again! The next

---

1   Not his real name.

day I came across a profile of a man who lived close to where my daughter Melissa lived. It took courage for me to express any interest because I kept hearing my mother say, "Don't run after boys!" I am a firm believer in men as initiators and women as responders. Call me old-fashioned, I guess.

So began an online friendship with Ed. We clicked right away, and our e-mails became longer, and more frequent. We had much in common and talked about many important things in our lives. Ed lived out of the country, but not so far that a plane ride couldn't bring us together in a few hours. I looked forward more and more to his waiting e-mails each day.

His words comforted me and awakened the hope of a relationship with a special man. Our e-mails were a place we could both share honestly, and openly. I became vulnerable and poured out my struggles and disappointments in my failed marriage, and my grief in losing Chrissie. We started talking over Skype and found that we enjoyed each other's company immensely. Soon we talked almost every day.

I felt that I was falling in love. I believed our meeting to be no accident and that God had brought us together. I prayed often that if this wasn't God's will for me, He would take this man out of my life. But we grew closer and closer as the weeks passed. We were both a little taken aback by the intensity of our feelings and how comfortable we felt with each other on Skype. We became best of friends, and talking with Ed became the highlight of my day. I think God accelerated our friendship, for He knew how much I needed the support and encouragement of this man through the coming crisis.

Chapter 8
Into the Fiery Furnace

"He trained us first, passed us like silver through refining fires."

(Psalm 66:12, MSG)

In June of 2015, as I took a Sabbath walk with Colleen, we discussed my health. I complained about my energy levels, and it suddenly dawned on me that I might be anemic. My periods had been heavy and irregular for quite some time. I wondered, "Perhaps I should go and see one of the Wildwood doctors on Monday." That same afternoon I noticed a new pain in my abdomen, unlike the cramps I usually experienced with the irregular bleeding. I mentioned the pain to Ed while talking with him on Skype that evening.

Looking up the symptoms of anemia, it all seemed to fit: fatigue; loss of energy; rapid heartbeat—especially with exercise; shortness of breath; leg cramps; insomnia. I probably would have delayed seeing a doctor even longer if I hadn't woken up that Monday morning, June 8, feeling strangely weak and shaky. I had to sit down in a chair while giving a guest a contrast shower in hydro. I decided to see one of our physicians right away.

By divine providence, Dr. N happened to be the only physician available. As the crisis unfolded, I knew I had the right doctor. She ordered bloodwork to check my hemoglobin levels and examined my abdomen. Her concern mounted as she felt a mass in my lower pelvic area and then found a sensitive area in my upper right abdomen. The blood test showed my hemoglobin levels to be 6.4, dangerously below the norm of 12. Dr. N sent me directly to the hospital emergency room for a blood transfusion and ordered a CT scan of my abdomen.

In an instant I plunged into a nightmare that I could not wake up from! Trevor and Colleen drove me to the hospital in Chattanooga and got me checked into the ER. I received two units of blood and a CT scan during the transfusion. I spent the whole night in the ER. Colleen and Trevor could not stay with me for long. They were travelling to Oregon the next day for their daughter Taryn's graduation from nursing school. I felt bereft as they finally left me alone in the ER at around 10:00 p.m. For my birthday two months earlier, Colleen and Trevor gave me a used iPhone, little knowing the impact this gift would have on my life. It became my lifeline to my parents and Kyle in South Africa, and to Melissa and Ed in Canada. Ed's support was invaluable, as he stayed texting with me until 1:30 a.m.

The ER doctor came to report that the scan showed a large mass in my uterus, probably a fibroid. "It most likely means a hysterectomy will not be needed." I questioned, "What about the other sensitive area in my abdomen?" He dismissed me with, "We didn't pick anything up." He also informed me that my iron levels were extremely low.

At 5:00 a.m. they moved me to a hospital room and gave me an iron transfusion. Later that morning I did a pelvic ultrasound and a contrast CT scan. I found the ultrasound excruciating, since the technician had to apply firm pressure to my stomach. Afterwards, my whole abdomen felt inflamed. With a contrast CT scan, iodine is injected through the IV to make the organs show up better. As the iodine entered my bloodstream I suddenly felt a burning hot sensation shooting from the back of my throat all the way down to my bladder!

In the afternoon a surgeon and a gynecologist came to see me. Their faces were solemn. "You have a large mass in your uterus and another one on your right adrenal gland. We are not sure whether they are related. We may possibly do a biopsy on the adrenal gland mass tomorrow." My mind could not deal with this information. I rested in bed the rest of the day and tried not to think. I felt a little better after the blood transfusion, although still weak and hurting after all the poking and prodding. I sent off a brief e-mail to my parents: "It's really hard going through all this without any family nearby, not even Colleen and Trevor. But God is my strength and He is holding me in His strong arms." As I talked with Ed on the phone that night, the pain eased considerably. I teased him, "You are good medicine for me!"

The next morning the lab drew my blood and gave me another iron transfusion. At lunchtime the doctors appeared at my bedside. "Your bloodwork looks good. Your hemoglobin is up to 8, so we are going to discharge you." They organized appointments for me to see the gynecologist and an endocrine doctor in two weeks' time. I left the hospital, in pain and feeling feverish.

On Thursday I still felt weak and shaky. I had an appointment with Dr. N in the afternoon and my pulse was 96—way too high. Dr. N had the lab draw blood again since she thought I might need another blood transfusion. She went over the hospital scan report with me and I finally got the full picture: a large mass (14 cm) in the uterus, enlarged lymph nodes in the abdomen, and a mass on the adrenal gland. Dr. N called the gynecologist during my appointment with her, anxious to start me on progesterone to stop the bleeding. The gynecologist spoke bluntly. "If it is cancer, the progesterone won't help, but you can try it anyway. I will probably do a complete hysterectomy. If it does turn out to be cancer, then I recommend radiation and possibly chemotherapy as well." My brain went numb. I refused to even entertain the thought that I might have cancer.

When I asked Dr. N her opinion on radiation and chemotherapy, she advised, "You need to pray about it and do what God tells you to do, not what everyone else says." At that moment I didn't even know how to think, let alone pray. My mind struggled to grasp the seriousness of my situation.

When Melissa heard the news she wanted to come and be with me, but her permanent residence for Canada had not yet been approved. Unable to leave the country without that approval, there seemed to be nothing she could do. She appealed to Canadian immigration to see if they could speed up the process, but to no avail. I longed to have her with me during this difficult time, but submitted to God's will, trusting that He was in control.

That night I had a serious talk with Ed. "I will understand if you can't handle all this and decide to end our relationship." His words reassured me. "What is happening to you doesn't scare me. I will be by your side all the way." His support gave me strength to fight. I had to get well so I could go and meet him in person!

The next day I woke up filled with hope. Exodus 14:14 came to my mind: "The Lord will fight for you, and you shall hold your peace" (NKJV). My energy levels felt better, and Dr. N reported that my hemoglobin levels were holding at 8. I wouldn't need another blood transfusion. I decided to watch some videos on YouTube about cancer cures. I came across a German doctor who stated that if a person raises the pH level in their body, cancer will disappear in two to sixteen weeks. He recommended going onto a raw food diet, as that's the quickest way to alkalize the body. I went on to watch inspiring testimonies of people who refused conventional medical treatment and cured their cancer with a raw food diet. I didn't know if I had cancer or not, but I began eating 100% raw foods. I took courage from this quote: "If anything is causing worry or anxiety, let us stop rehearsing the difficulty and trust God for healing, love and power."[2]

Unsure why God had given me a two-week delay before seeing the gynecologist again, I began praying for a miracle. God said we don't have because we don't ask (James 4:2), so I asked big. "Lord, help my body to shrink these masses so that I won't even need surgery, let alone radiation or chemotherapy." I worked on my mental attitude and clung to God, rejecting any negative or fearful thoughts. I felt helpless, in over my head. I believed in God's health laws, but had never before put them to the test as I did now. I cast my helpless soul on Him and trusted Him to take care of me.

> *I felt helpless, in over my head. I believed in God's health laws, but had never before put them to the test as I did now.*

The following Monday, one week after I had first been admitted to the hospital, I took a turn for the worse. Bleeding heavily again, I felt weak and dizzy. The pain became intense. I wasn't even sure I could walk the short distance to the Lifestyle Center Clinic to see the doctor. One of the clinic nurses came to check my vitals at my apartment. When they consulted with Dr. N, she expressed concern about my hemoglobin level and mentioned the possibility of another blood transfusion. She decided to send me back to the ER. Dr. N confessed later, "I wasn't sure if I made the right call in sending you to the ER again, and prayed earnestly about it." As it turned out, she made the right decision. When the ER doctor examined me, he confirmed, "You need to have surgery as soon as possible." Once again they admitted me to the hospital.

The following morning the endocrine doctor came to explain the situation to me. "The best scenario is that these are two totally unrelated benign masses that can be removed with no trouble. However, we first have to determine whether or not the adrenal mass is an adrenalin-producing tumor. If it is, it could cause problems during surgery, so we would have to deal with it first. If we deal with the uterine mass first and it turns out to be cancerous, we would probably do a PET scan to determine if the

---

2   *Review and Herald,* Oct 7, 1965.

adrenal mass is cancerous too. The first step is to do a twenty-four-hour urine test, and then we can take it from there."

Later, a gynecologist came to talk with me. He informed me that after the urine test they were going to do a D&C to try to remove the mass from my uterus and see what we were dealing with. With compassion in his voice he reassured me, "Don't worry, I'll take good care of you." He explained that if the mass was benign he would be happy to remove my uterus and there would be no reason why I shouldn't be able to keep my ovaries. "However, the growth is sitting right in the middle of your uterus, and if it's soft enough, I might be able to break it up and pull it out." That would mean no surgery! He added that the enlarged lymph nodes didn't necessarily mean cancer. I clung to the hope that this would be the case. The doctor prescribed pain medication for my IV and hormones to stop the bleeding. After the pain meds took effect my body relaxed. I felt like I had been in labor 24/7 the past few days and was exhausted.

On my way down to the operating room for the D&C I committed myself into God's hands. When I woke up in the recovery room, Colleen and Trevor were there to see me. I felt immensely comforted to have them back. I didn't see the doctor, so I had no idea what he had found, but I felt at peace.

The doctor called me that evening. "I didn't want you to be wondering all night. What I saw did not look to me like endometrial cancer. It looked more like fibroids that grew too big for their blood supply and started to break down. But we need to wait for the pathology results tomorrow to be sure. I removed a cup of blood and tissue from your uterus, which was enlarged to about the size of a four-to-five-month pregnancy. If the results are good I will let you go home and give your body a chance to recover. Then we can take it from there." I messaged my parents, "Praise God for hope so far!" I pleaded with God for it not to be cancer, but the thought nagged in the back of my mind, "What about the mass on the adrenal gland?"

The next day, June 19, I received a phone call. "I'm sorry, Ms. McLeod, but it *was* cancer." My whole body went numb. Unbelief and confusion overwhelmed me. How could this be? A third tragedy in my life, none of which I had ever expected to happen to me. Another of those moments when I did not like my life at all, but felt helpless to do anything about it. I clung to the words that my friend, Jodi, gave me: "Above the distractions of the earth He sits enthroned; all things are opened to His divine survey; and from His great and calm eternity He orders that which providence sees best."[3] I had to believe that God was in control.

---

3   White, *The Ministry of Healing*, p. 417.

I shared the news with my family, in shock and devastated that none of them could be with me. Melissa spent a great deal of time with me on Skype that day. When I talked with Ed he reassured me that this changed nothing in our relationship. My parents had only encouraging words for me: "Do not give up praying and holding on to Jesus, for He is faithful and will go ahead and fight for you. God is preparing you for big things, grounding you in such a deep and lasting faith, that you will never be moved. This is the faith He will give you and use you to show His glory, His character, to give a powerful testimony of His love for you. Wait, my girl, wait and see what the Lord will do for you."

After the cancer diagnosis, wheels were set in motion by the hospital, and I felt swept up into a forward momentum that I was powerless to control. But I know that God never let go of the wheel and orchestrated everything according to His perfect plan.

The doctors decided that I needed to have surgery as soon as possible. I had to stay in the hospital until my surgery date, which they scheduled for Friday, June 26. The next few days were a blur of meeting surgeons, anesthetists, and doctors. My surgery required two surgeons—one to do a hysterectomy, and the other to do an adrenalectomy. Before surgery I had to go for a chest CT scan, and receive two units of blood.

A few days later they informed me that my surgery had been rescheduled for two days earlier, and that a different surgeon would do the hysterectomy. When I met Dr. Todd Boren, I understood why God wanted me to have this man as my surgeon. The first doctor to actually sit down on the end of my bed, he gave me his time and full attention. He explained in detail what they needed to do as far as the surgery went. "I plan to do a robotic hysterectomy, which only entails a few small holes in your abdomen. But if I cannot see clearly, I will have to make an incision and open you up. I will do a radical hysterectomy, which means removing your uterus, ovaries, cervix, and affected lymph nodes in that area. I will do the hysterectomy first, and then the other surgeon will come in and remove your adrenal gland."

When we discussed the plan after surgery, Dr. Boren told me I would probably require both chemotherapy and radiation. Everything inside me rebelled at the thought. As Dr. Boren explained the treatments and the side effects, my first thought was, "I don't want to lose all my hair." Vanity perhaps, but God used my vanity to strengthen my resolve! My previous experiences with my mom and chemotherapy and my son and radiation immediately came to mind. I remembered how I always told myself that if

I ever got cancer I would never have chemotherapy or radiation. I believed I knew a better way. My studies in health had convinced me.

So I told Dr. Boren, "I want to treat my cancer with lifestyle only." Colleen happened to be with me that day and she explained to Dr. Boren what we did at Wildwood. At one point, Dr. Boren asked Colleen, "Does Wildwood have success treating lymphedema?" Colleen replied, "No, we don't seem to be able to do much to help with that." At the time I had no idea what lymphedema was and didn't even want to ask, as I had already been bombarded with way too much scary information. I guess Dr. Boren knew that I would most likely face lymphedema after surgery (swelling of my legs due to the loss of lymph nodes), but perhaps he could see that I had heard enough, for he didn't go into any further detail.

I recognized God's providence when Dr. Boren told us of his deep interest in the connection between disease and lifestyle. He had read *The China Study* and watched *Forks Over Knives*, and dialogued with Dr. Colin Campbell, one of the authors of *The China Study*. However, he stated that even though he believed lifestyle could help with cancer, he did not believe that it could cure. "If you refuse chemotherapy and radiation, I am only willing to do palliative surgery—in other words, just remove your uterus to prevent you from bleeding to death." My heart sank. I promised him, "I will think about it and let you know." After he left I felt confused and scared. What should I do?

When Dr. Boren returned to see me the following day, I timidly questioned, "Do you still only want to do palliative surgery if I refuse treatment?" I believe God had been working on his heart.

"No, I've changed my mind. I will do the surgery and remove every trace of cancer I can find. I will support you in the path you are choosing—be your partner. I want to believe that lifestyle works, but I've never seen proof. I would love to be 'high-fiving' with you in my office in five years' time! However, realize this: with the seriousness of your condition, you only have one shot at this." But one shot is all God needs! I clung to that hope.

My mom put me in touch with a pastor friend in South Africa. A number of years previously, he fought his own battle with cancer and won, using God's simple laws of health. He e-mailed and encouraged me, and gave two specific instructions which I felt were God-directed. The first instruction was to be anointed without delay, and to commit my life and my healing to God. Secondly, he told me to claim Jeremiah 30:17: "I will give you back your health again and heal your wounds." That verse has become a part of me, and I still remind God every single day of His promise!

I asked Trevor and Colleen to speak to the chaplain at the Lifestyle Center and arrange an anointing service for me. On June 22, Pastor Steve, Trevor and Colleen, and Vaughan and Magda (the president of Wildwood and his wife, also good friends of mine from South Africa) came to my hospital room. I will never forget the peace I felt that day as I committed myself into God's hands and trusted Him with my healing. The anointing service was beautiful. Vaughan prayed a bold prayer, asking God to heal me even before surgery. "But we have to say Thy will be done." Then Pastor Steve prayed and placed the oil on my forehead. I felt calm after they left. However, the enemy got busy the next morning and I woke up terrified. I prayed desperately for God to help me. Colleen visited me early every morning and she stayed longer than usual with me this time. I told my parents, "I'm praying for a miracle. There are still twenty-four hours before surgery. But I have to submit to God's will. I want God to be glorified in everything that happens."

The adrenal tests came back normal, and everything went ahead as planned. The night before surgery I e-mailed my parents: "Busy drinking magnesium citrate right now so guess the bathroom run will start soon, cleaning me out for surgery! Liquids only from now till midnight and then nothing by mouth at all. Still praying for a miracle but staying in God's loving arms no matter what happens."

June 24, 2015, the day of my surgery, arrived. It happened to be Colleen's birthday, and she chose to spend it with me in the hospital. How I appreciated her sacrifice! With my family thousands of miles away, unable to be with me, I felt so alone. But God, Who had made every provision for me through this crisis, gave me a wonderful "sister" in Colleen. Her support meant the world to me. I talked with Ed that morning. In retrospect, I feel selfish for the way I simply expected him to be there for me. I cannot imagine how he must have felt. As he commented later, "The picture just kept getting worse and worse."

My nerves were on edge all morning in anticipation of my surgery. Once again, I felt trapped in this nightmare with no escape. I had a sense of being led where I did not want to go, as John 21:18 says: "You will stretch out your hands, and someone else will get you ready to take you where you don't want to go" (GW). I had so hoped that God would heal me before the surgery. But He had another plan. I pleaded with Him over and over again to be with me and to give me His peace. Committing myself to Him once more, I told Him, "If I don't wake up from the surgery, that's OK with me. I trust You with my life."

When the moment came to be taken down to the surgical floor, I felt God's peace fill my heart. Colleen accompanied me to be prepped for surgery, staying with me as long as she could. I expected the surgery to be routine, over in three-to-four hours, without the necessity of a major incision in my abdomen. As I lost consciousness in the operating room, God's presence enveloped me.

Chapter 9

In the Valley of the Shadow

"Even when walking through the dark valley of death I will not be afraid, for you are close beside me, guarding, guiding all the way."

(Psalm 23:4)

"Good morning, Ms. McLeod. Its 6:00 a.m. and you're in the ICU."

The nurse's voice pierced the fog of anesthetic. Amid the beeping of machines and the bustle all around me, I tried to focus my eyes. My mind raced. What am I doing here? What has happened? My surgery began at 2:45 p.m. yesterday—where did all that time go? Thus began the darkest moments of my life, moments where I clung to my Jesus with every ounce of strength in my wounded and bruised body.

The nurse explained that my surgery had lasted almost eight hours, and I had been sedated and on the ventilator all night. Why did the surgery take so long? She instructed me, "You are still connected to the breathing tube, but before we can remove it, you need to breathe through the tube for at least one hour. We have to be sure you can breathe on your own." Extremely weak after the surgery, I found it difficult to take the deep breaths necessary to get enough oxygen into my lungs. As I fought for every breath I thought for sure it would be my last. I felt exhausted but too terrified to fall asleep for fear I would stop breathing.

That hour felt like an eternity. I prayed constantly, desperately, "Lord, please help me to take my next breath." In those moments God reminded me of 1 Peter 4:12, 13, which says, "Don't feel as though something strange is happening to you, but be happy as you share Christ's sufferings" (GW). Jesus tenderly spoke these thoughts into my mind, "This is how I felt as I hung dying on the cross—fighting for every breath. It is a privilege to suffer as I suffered. I am with you and will never let you go."

The worst moment of all came with the removal of the breathing tube. I had huge grey mitts on my hands to prevent me from grabbing hold of the tube. I can understand why they do that. As they slowly removed the tube I could not take a breath and thought I would die. Panicking, I tried to fight. "Stop it!" the nurse harshly barked. What a relief when that tube finally came out!

Not long after that Colleen, Trevor, and their daughter Taryn came to see me. Still groggy and with a sore throat from the breathing tube, I tried to talk. But they couldn't hear what I said. Colleen explained, "Your surgery only ended at about 11:00 p.m. last night. We stayed up until we heard you would be OK." None of us understood yet what had transpired in that operating room. I will never forget the comfort Colleen gave me that morning. While they visited with me, she stood by my side and gently stroked my arm.

As bad timing would have it again, Colleen and Trevor had to leave on a business trip the next day. They promised that Taryn would come and visit me every day, which she faithfully did. I spent two days in the ICU, and finally pieced together what happened during the surgery. Dr. Boren found the cancer to be more extensive than he expected and had to resort to open surgery. A letter which Dr. N later wrote at the request of Melissa, in an attempt to make some headway with Canadian immigration, gives the full picture of how desperate my situation was. Could it have been any worse?

Alison McLeod is a 49 y/o female who has been under my care since early June, 2015. She was diagnosed with stage IVB endometrial cancer with the rarely encountered adrenal gland metastasis (four cases described in the medical literature). It is stage IVB because the cancer involved her cervix, ovaries, the lining of the tissues that hold the abdominal organs in place (omentum), extensive lymph nodes including distant lymph nodes, abdominal fluid and, as mentioned, the adrenal gland. Unfortunately, despite the extensive dissection done during the surgery, the margins of the tissues that were resected still had microscopic tumor cells seen on biopsy, suggesting that there are still cancer cells present in her body. She is status post a 7+ hour surgery on June 24, 2015 aimed at debulking the tumor (initial exploratory laparotomy converted to open surgery: radical abdominal hysterectomy, bilateral salpingo-oopherectomy, bilateral pelvic and extensive para-aortic lymph node dissection, cystoscopy, left ureterolysis and right adrenalectomy). As much of the visible tumor as could be seen was removed. Alison did not have the typical risk factors associated with endometrial cancer. She has been diagnosed at an early age (atypical) with such extensive cancer likely secondary to the expression of a gene found on her cancer cells associated with Lynch Syndrome, an aggressive form of endometrial cancer.

I discovered that I had an incision from "stem to stern," as one of the nurses put it. The area of the incision just below my breastbone gave me much discomfort. I felt as if I had a band across my ribs and could not breathe deeply. I admitted to the nurse, "I'm scared to fall asleep because I feel like I'm going to stop breathing." She offered to sit with me for a while and watch my breathing while I slept. When I woke up she reassured me, "You were breathing just fine." Despite the powerful pain meds, I experienced tremendous pain. Flat on my back, every hour or two the nurses came and shifted my position with pillows towards the left side or the right. This felt excruciating and I braced myself every time they walked into my room.

On the second day in the ICU the physical therapist made me sit up in a chair. I thought I would die, or at least all of my insides would fall out! I hated feeling so helpless. I've always been healthy and independent, and even after my C-sections got back on my feet within a day or two. Having feared doctors, hospitals, and needles all my life, I had been thrown into my worst nightmare! I got poked every day to have my blood checked, and during my stay in the hospital I must have had at least ten different IVs in my arms. Feeling like a pin-cushion, my arms were black and blue.

After two days in the ICU they removed the catheter and transferred me to a room in the oncology ward. From the time I went into surgery Colleen stayed in touch with my family, giving them regular updates on my condition. She continued to do this even while she was away, passing on news from Taryn, until I had been settled in the oncology ward and started using my phone again. My parents were understandably concerned and Colleen patiently answered all their questions. My mom e-mailed Colleen,

"Please thank Taryn for all she is doing for our precious daughter. We are praying that she can go home soon, and be in a beautiful environment, with loving people around her. Thanks for listening, and understanding our concerns. We are putting her in God's hands, and know He is looking after her, but I guess we are human to be concerned. We are so far away! Thanks for your wonderful support of Alison. We are deeply thankful!"

In the oncology ward I needed help every time I went to the bathroom. In addition to receiving IV fluids in my arm, I still had the arterial IV just below my collar-bone, through which the nurses administered the pain meds. I found climbing in and out of bed and walking with such a huge incision difficult to say the least. Every shift change the nurses checked the incision and the five holes in my sides where the robot had been placed. On my left side I had a stomach drain which needed emptying constantly.

For days I could not bring myself to look at my incision. When I finally plucked up the courage, to my amazement I discovered that I had no stitches on the outside. I had been glued closed! It took me months to finally get all the glue peeled off my skin, but it certainly held me together!

They kept me on a liquid diet for a few days, but when I tried solid foods, my body rebelled. The trauma from the surgery, and the extremely strong pain meds (stronger than morphine) totally paralyzed my digestive system. When I ate, the food sat in my stomach and made me nauseous. The doctor tried me on one round of laxative after another, but nothing helped.

Grotesquely swollen from the hips down, I feared I would look that way forever. On July 1, I e-mailed my parents, "I'm sorry for not e-mailing. I've had two bad days. Still in the hospital. Struggling with pain, nausea, and constipation. Also bad swelling in the hips and legs. Doctors say it's because my lymph nodes are gone. More x-rays and ultrasounds. Want this to be over now. Don't know when I'll be going home. Please pray hard. Struggling emotionally. Wish Melissa could be here."

Those eleven post-surgery days in the hospital were a blur of needles, nausea, pain, and fear. I felt terrible and looked terrible and didn't want to see anyone, apart from Taryn and my friend, Jodi. Taryn came faithfully twice a day and helped me with simple tasks which I now found challenging, such as washing my hair and taking walks down the hallway. Jodi and I had been friends ever since she came as a guest on one of our Wildwood lifestyle programs. She never failed to cheer me up with her sense of humor. The visits from these two were bright spots in my days. Ed and I texted and talked on the phone every day. His friendship gave me a reason to hold on to life.

Five days after the surgery I finally received a visit from Dr. Boren. His words were sobering. "It was bad. The cancer was everywhere. I had to peel it off of your organs and from around your aorta. I almost gave up. But I removed everything I could find. What you have is extremely aggressive and I *strongly* recommend radiation." With my thoughts in turmoil, I e-mailed my parents, "Just saw the surgeon and he said he removed a lot of the tumor from my body. He is recommending radiation, along with the aggressive diet I want to follow. I hate the thought of radiation but I'm scared. I need to know what God wants me to do. Please pray for me. I don't know what to do."

> *"It was bad. The cancer was everywhere. I had to peel it off of your organs and from around your aorta. I almost gave up.*

By July 4, I still had not left the hospital. My stomach refused to tolerate anything more than liquids. The nausea had improved somewhat, due to anti-nausea medication. The last thing I wanted to do was throw up and open my incision! My legs and feet were still swollen but my mobility improved daily, as I persevered with the walks down the hallway. I continued to need the heavy pain medication. Trying to last as long as I could, after four or five hours I had to ask for more. The intense pain throbbed and burned throughout my whole abdomen. As the nurse injected the medication into my IV, I felt a strange shakiness in my stomach, and then blissful relief as the drug took effect. Finding it hard to concentrate on anything, I spent much of the time dozing. I had to force myself to get up and walk a few times a day, as the temptation to stay dozing and escape the nightmare of my reality felt overwhelming. My mind simply could not wrap itself around all that had happened. Numbness was a blessing.

I will never forget the night I had to be weaned off the IV pain meds and onto the oral form, in preparation for discharge from the hospital. The oral meds were much less effective than the IV meds and I could only get the meds every four hours. In between I had to deal with the pain. For the first time I experienced the excruciating pain from my surgery, unmasked by the IV pain meds. I had an older male nurse that night, and he did his best to console me, as I writhed and moaned. "Women are strong and you are handling the pain so well. If it had been me, I would have been screaming!" At around 2:00 a.m. the pain felt intolerable, and

I cried out to God, "Please help me because I can't take any more!" I sat up on the side of the bed and did deep breathing and much praying, and the pain finally eased.

Before my surgery Dr. Boren assured me, "You can stay in the hospital as long as you need to. We aren't going to kick you out." Strange as it may sound, I clung to what he said. When it actually came down to it, leaving the hospital scared me. With all the difficulties after the surgery, I felt safe in the hospital, with nurses and doctors close at hand. I feared I wouldn't be able to cope when I got home. Each time the doctors postponed my discharge, I felt a sense of relief that I wouldn't have to deal with the real world just yet.

I eventually left the hospital on July 6, 2015. As he discharged me, Dr. Boren's partner warned, "You have to have chemotherapy. The cancer is going to come back anyway, but you have to have chemotherapy." That did not make sense to me. "There is no way I'm having chemotherapy," I thought. I later discovered that the doctors did not expect me to survive more than six months.

The nurses removed the last IV, and slowly pulled out the stomach drain—an extremely painful procedure, leaving me with a small hole in my abdomen. Just another scar to add to my collection! It felt strange to get dressed after weeks of wearing green hospital gowns. Still swollen from the surgery, the skirt I had worn to the hospital felt tight around my waist. My feet did not fit into my shoes, so I put on my slippers. I feared that none of my clothes and shoes would ever fit me again and I would be misshapen for the rest of my life. Taryn arrived to fetch me and helped to pack up my belongings. Weak and scared, ready or not, it was time to go home.

Chapter 10
Walking in Sunshine

**"Nature's process of healing and upbuilding is gradual,
and to the impatient it seems slow."**

(Ellen White, *The Ministry of Healing*, p. 127)

Colleen and Trevor had not yet returned. However, they graciously offered to have Taryn take care of me in their home for the first few days after leaving the hospital. There is no way I would have managed going back to my apartment all alone. I appreciated Taryn's help in changing the dressing for my stomach drain wound and giving me daily blood thinner shots. I could probably have changed the dressing myself, but it grossed me out and I am a baby when it comes to that type of thing. The Wildwood Diet Kitchen, by order of Dr. N, began preparing green juices and raspberry walnut smoothies for me, and Taryn collected them from the Lifestyle Center. I struggled to eat, and survived those first days on the juices and smoothies. Losing ten pounds in one week, and thirty pounds altogether before my weight stabilized, I seemed to be swimming in all my clothes. One day I put on one of my skirts for the first time since surgery and it dropped straight to the floor! Amused, I chuckled, "Wow, I've never had this problem before!"

A day or two after arriving home, Taryn drove me up to the Lifestyle Center for an appointment with Dr. N. She received me with compassion and gentleness. "Do you want to do chemo or radiation?" I shook my head. "Then I will fully support you in putting every effort into fighting this with lifestyle." She worked out a simple program for me to follow, which I appreciated, as even that seemed overwhelming to me.

Dr. N advised me to consider compression stockings for the swelling in my legs, and that I may need a long-term stocking, given the loss of lymph nodes. "However, the swelling could also have been caused by all the blood transfusions you had, as the blood has a tendency to pool." I needed to stick with the green juices and smoothies until my digestive system sorted itself out, but eventually my goal would be 60–80% raw foods. However, my brain and muscles needed well-cooked whole grains and legumes. "Use plenty of garlic and onions, and remember, berries and beets are your friends." I had to drink four cups of a specialized tea per day, plus at least six cups of water, and start taking turmeric capsules. My vitamin D levels were almost non-existent, so I needed to take a supplement. For exercise I had to work up to walking one hour a day, seven days a week, and to eventually incorporate weight-bearing exercises.

Dr. N instructed me to decrease my pain medication only as I felt able to function. "Being in too much pain hinders the healing process," she explained. I hated being on the pain medication as it made me dopey and slowed my digestion. But the pain was still severe, especially at night. I felt a sense of purpose after talking with Dr. N and putting a plan in place. Going home with Taryn, I began following these simple instructions as best I could. I felt overwhelmed at times with all the things I wanted to be doing and could not because my digestive system refused to cooperate. I had to simply trust that God had His hand over me.

The first miracle happened with the lymphedema that remained in my right leg and foot. On the Friday after I left the hospital, Dr. N came to the house and showed me how to wrap my foot and leg with a tight ACE® bandage. She advised me, "Keep it on during the day and take it off when you go to bed at night. This may help with the swelling." I kept the bandage on for the rest of that afternoon, and took it off at bedtime. When I woke up the next morning, the swelling had disappeared, and it never came back! I couldn't believe it! I rejoiced in God's goodness and mercy towards me.

I felt a little stronger each day. What a blessing to be back in the beauty and peace of the country setting at Wildwood. There is something so healing about being out in God's creation. I believe walking played a huge part in my recovery. I walked along the road by Colleen and Trevor's house as much as I could each day. I needed Taryn's help to get up and down the step on the front porch, but I walked consistently, especially after meals. Dr. N prescribed a digestive walk of at least ten to fifteen minutes after each meal. It helped tremendously with the discomfort I felt after eating. My stomach went into a spasm every time I put anything in it, even water. If I sat or lay down after eating, I felt even worse.

Seeing Ed on Skype again brought healing to my soul. I didn't want him to see me in the hospital, for I felt and looked terrible. My vanity surfaced again. One of the first things I did when I got home from the hospital was color my hair—before I talked to Ed on Skype! Taryn obligingly helped me, as I could barely lift my arms. She probably thought me a little crazy, but humored me anyway. Talking with Ed every day gave me something to look forward to and helped me feel a sense of normalcy. I asked him seriously one day, "Why do you stay with me? Many other men would bail out if something like this happened." The only way he knew how to explain it related to how he felt as a firefighter. "When everyone else is running out of the burning building, I am running in! I believe in friendship and loyalty. What is happening to you doesn't scare me. I want to be here for you." I felt blessed to have him in my life.

One week after leaving the hospital the time came to vacate Colleen and Trevor's bedroom and return to my own apartment. I felt nervous about coping on my own, since simply taking a shower exhausted me. I couldn't bend over and still found getting in and out of bed a challenge. I had no idea how I would clean my apartment. But God moved me into this little home six months before I got sick, and prepared everything I needed. I lived right behind the Lifestyle Center, with a ramp going up to the side door. I didn't even have to climb stairs to get to my hydro or doctor's appointments. Lifestyle staff delivered the freshly made green juices right to my door. I was also only a few steps away from the Guest Services office, where I soon began working for an hour or two a day. I did not have the strength to go back to working in hydro yet. I felt safe with my Wildwood family so close by.

I began receiving hydrotherapy for pain and the healing of my incision—moist, hot fomentations for twenty minutes every day. I found it quite an adjustment being the patient instead of the therapist! Later, after my incision healed up and the pain lessened, I received the Russian steam bath as a heat treatment and for detoxing. This treatment is comparable to a steam sauna. To this day I still try to do the Russian steam bath at least once a week. Dr. N also prescribed lower back massage for the constipation. I have since then continued to have back or leg massages—the leg massages helping, I believe, to improve the circulation in my legs.

Colleen lent me a heating pad which I used often during the day to help with the pain. As soon as the pain became manageable, I tried to get through the night on Tylenol® instead of the strong narcotic I had been using. Colleen made me charcoal poultices which I put over my liver at night for a couple of weeks, to help with detoxing. Dr. N demonstrated her compassion by checking on me often, assuring me I could call or text her any time of the day or night. I had many questions and she patiently answered them all. Her passionate prayers with me pleaded for healing and for wisdom for both of us. She encouraged me, "You are doing amazingly well compared to other patients I know who have been through similar surgery."

My body responded to the juices, hydrotherapy and massage, walking, sunshine, and the love from family and friends poured out upon me. On July 20 Colleen messaged my parents: "I went to visit Alison late yesterday and we took a long walk. I was amazed at how well she did! God is certainly blessing her efforts to get well!" I trusted in God's healing power, but I believe I needed to demonstrate my faith by my works, by cooperating with everything God showed me to do. The pain began to ease, and I grew stronger every day. My digestive system recovered and Wildwood graciously allowed me to get my meals from the Diet Kitchen. This lifted the burden of having to worry about what I should eat.

However, my recovery did not come without its challenges. The constipation was a nightmare. But as I tolerated more solid foods, and ate the wonderful, healthy, fiber-filled, mostly raw, vegan food that the Diet Kitchen provided, it soon became a thing of the past.

Shortly after I moved back home I began experiencing tachycardia, with a heart rate of over 100. My usual heart rate had been in the 70–80s. It mystified Dr. N because I felt fine, and could even continue exercising. I had traces of blood in my urine, probably related to the surgical procedures that had been done. Since tachycardia can be related to infection, I took a course of antibiotics in case I had a urinary tract infection. Dr. N also sent me for a CT scan of my lungs, in case I had a blood clot. The nurse tried four times before she could get an IV in for the contrast. My veins were full of scar tissue from all the IV's I had in the hospital. During this procedure I battled the fear that I had a clot and that the nightmare of hospitals and doctors would continue. God spoke words of comfort to me in that moment, through a Bible verse stuck up on the cubicle of the lady who registered me for the scan: "I have heard your prayer, I have seen your tears; surely I will heal you" (2 Kings 20:5, NKJV).

The scan showed no blood clot. However, the tachycardia persisted. Dr. N did an EKG, which showed my heart to be fine. Eventually, after a few weeks it resolved itself, and now, with all the exercise I do, I have a heart rate of under 60! It is a mystery to this day, but who knows what chemical changes my body experienced as it adjusted to the loss of my ovaries and one of my adrenal glands?

Not long after I left the hospital, I shared with Colleen for the first time about my emotional battle, particularly the fear which stalked me. I confided, "Sometimes I find it impossible to concentrate on praying or reading my Bible."

She reminded me, "God understands and during those times you can simply rest in Him. But when the scary thoughts come, text me and I will pray for you, or come and be with you if you need me!" She encouraged me to start a "gratitude journal" and write down each day what I could be thankful for. Beginning right away, it surprised me to see how many blessings I came up with!

One weekend I watched a DVD on dealing with fear, anxiety, and stress. The speaker instructed, "Write all your fears and worries down, then take them to God in prayer and give them to Him. Destroy the piece of paper and when the devil comes to torment you with a certain fear tell him you don't have it any more—God does!" So that is what I did. There were times I forgot to give my fears to God, but when I eventually remembered to pray instead of worry, He gave me His perfect peace. He enabled me to hold on to hope. I wrote to my parents, "I know my case looks hopeless to the medical world, but with God nothing is impossible."

At times my health program seemed to have taken over my life. I tried to faithfully follow everything Dr. N told me to do. But it felt as though I spent my days walking, drinking, swallowing supplements, and sleeping! I started going to bed at 7:30 p.m., as I knew I needed plenty of rest. Thankfully, I soon figured out a routine that worked, and my health program became a part of me—something that I will continue for the rest of my life.

I talked with Ed every day and his support encouraged me. He assured me, "You look nice," even though I had never been skinnier. He cracked jokes to cheer me up and made me feel normal and loved. We longed to meet each other in person.

Six weeks after surgery, Dr. N was pleased with my progress. "I have seen patients this far out from surgery back in the hospital with infections, unable to eat or walk." I walked more than an hour a day, ate well, and had no more trouble with constipation. My mobility improved significantly. I found myself doing things without thinking, like standing up without having to push myself off the chair, or bending down to pick something up, or climbing into the car without hanging on. Then I realized, "Hey, I didn't even think about my stomach muscles!" The one thing that still bothered me was sitting for too long. I also couldn't stand up straight when I first got up because of the scar tissue on my abdomen. I continued to experience pain there, but it became less intense and less frequent.

On July 30, I went for my first follow-up appointment with Dr. Boren. I felt extremely nervous, and asked Colleen to go in with me. She took a pen and paper and made notes of everything Dr. Boren said so I could remember it afterwards. Dr. N wrote a letter for me to take to him, explaining everything that had happened with me since the surgery. She spoke about the natural program I followed and mentioned that I did not want to do chemo and radiation. Dr. Boren took a few moments to read the letter. Then he examined my incision briefly and did a pelvic exam. He said he would not do a biopsy, since I refused treatment. "However, I believe that the cancer is already growing again, because the type you have is very aggressive." He told me that I am a rare case. "I have never seen this type of cancer go to the adrenal gland, or affect so many lymph nodes. You are also atypical, being so young." Apparently twenty-one out of the twenty-six lymph nodes he removed were positive for cancer. He urged me to do chemo and radiation, and explained in detail all the pros and cons of the treatments. "However," he warned, "no matter what you do, this disease *will* take your life."

Colleen and I both concluded that chemo and radiation would not make much of a difference to my situation. Up until this point I had been uncertain, but now I decided once and for all that I would rather take a chance on God's way than on man's way. When I informed Dr. Boren of my decision, he did not put any pressure on me. Before we left he mentioned that I tested positive for the possibility that I carry the hereditary genetic mutation called Lynch Syndrome. This put me at extremely high risk for uterine and colon cancer. He recommended I inform my children and siblings of this, as they could be carrying the same gene. I left Dr. Boren's office shaken and scared, yet settled in my decision not to do chemo or radiation.

In the letter Dr. N wrote for Melissa she stated, "Current therapy recommendations discussed between the patient and her ob-gyn surgeon are such that the risks outweigh the benefits as presented to the patient and do not improve her survival rate enough for the patient to be willing to take on those risks and, as mentioned, cannot guarantee any improvement."

And so my course was set.

Chapter 11
Johana

"You use steel to sharpen steel, and one friend sharpens another."

(Proverbs 27:17, MSG)

By divine appointment, Johana received the assignment to give me hydrotherapy and massage treatments. Twenty-eight-years old and originally from Colombia, but now living in Argentina, she came to Wildwood to do the six-month medical missionary training course. Johana began working in hydro right at the time I went into the hospital. We met for the first time when I came for treatment after surgery. She is no stranger to suffering, having lost her father at the age of fourteen. He was kidnapped and they haven't seen him since. A physical therapist and respiratory therapist, Johana worked with many end-stage cancer patients and watched them die. She fought often with the doctors in the hospital in Argentina because they continued giving chemotherapy and radiation to the patients, even when they saw they were dying. Meeting Johana proved to be no coincidence.

I felt a special bond with Johana but only understood why later. She told me from the beginning that God brought her to Wildwood to meet me, and that she would tell me the reason someday. "Someday" came a few months later, and she shared the heartbreaking story of her best friend, Angie, who died the previous year from cancer. "I pleaded with her not to do chemotherapy, and to try the natural ways that I was convinced would help her. But the doctors scared her into doing chemotherapy." Johana spent every moment she could with her friend, even shaving her head in sympathy when Angie's hair fell out. Angie lost the battle and left Johana heartbroken. After Angie died, Johana asked God not to allow her death to be in vain: "Please give me a second chance to see that Your ways do work." God brought her to Wildwood and into my life. She fully supported the course I chose because she believed in it with all her heart. I desperately needed that support as I began my healing journey.

Johana found it difficult seeing my scars for the first time. They were exactly like Angie's, right down to the scar where the stomach drain had been. She later confided, "When I met you that day and prepared to give you your first hydrotherapy treatment, I knew you had just had surgery. But I had no idea what type of surgery or that you were

I felt a special bond with Johana but only understood why later. She told me from the beginning that God brought her to Wildwood to meet me, and that she would tell me the reason someday.

going through exactly what Angie did. When I found out I was in shock! And when you told me that you were choosing to heal God's way and wanted Him to have the glory, I said to myself, 'This is it! This is the answer to my prayer!'"

Now I knew why she understood me so well. Every fear and struggle I faced, she had gone through with Angie. God always gave her the right words for me at the right time, and her spiritual insight and maturity were way beyond her years. She became my greatest encourager. Johana wrote out a special Bible verse for me every time I went for my hydro treatments and her prayers for me were sincere and personal. That quiet time in hydro with Johana every afternoon became a safe haven from the scary world I had been plunged into.

Johana insisted that God was healing her heart through being able to work with me. We often argued about who received the greater blessing! She assured me, "I remember the day I begged Him for another chance to be a witness of His true ways of healing. I now have no doubt that you are that answered prayer. Thank you for being God's instrument to show me He is real and that He cares about our sorrows. Thank you for helping Him to heal the wounds of losing Angie."

When I had doubts about my healing, Johana was emphatic. "Trust me, you do *not* look like a cancer patient! I know you are fine. I see God's power working in you. He has a work for you to do. It has already begun." She felt my body growing stronger day by day beneath her hands as she gave me massages. God made every provision for my healing, even bringing a precious girl all the way from Argentina to minister to me. The thought overwhelmed me. Johana told me more than once, "If I came to Wildwood just to meet you, then it is enough."

Looking back, I am amazed at the way God brought special people into my life for a short window of time, exactly when I needed them. Johana only stayed at Wildwood for one year, but it was the most crucial year for me. Shortly after Johana left Wildwood and returned to Argentina, she shared with me the whole story of her journey to Wildwood. It thrilled me to see how God orchestrated our meeting:

We will eternally argue about who is a blessing to whom. I think about how I felt in Argentina, less than a month after Angie died, desperate and believing that life had no value at all. How could God have a purpose for me if we are so fragile and weak? Angie, a completely healthy woman, died in such a miserable way, destroyed. I didn't want to live without a purpose. I knew His ways were perfect but felt that I had no way to prove that they worked. I believed they would have if Angie had chosen to follow them and believe in what God says and not men. I felt I would never have a chance to experience it and see it with my own eyes. I cried and cried, wanting to die and no longer feel such pain. I did not know that He would answer my desperate prayer months later in His perfect timing.

Wildwood came to my mind. I went there the year before to see it and I didn't like it. But now I felt like it would be a good way to escape from all the familiar places that brought back so many memories. I couldn't face the reality that Angie wasn't there anymore. After crying and fasting for a week, I decided to apply to Wildwood without saying a word to anyone. I wanted this to be between God and me. A week after applying, my mom texted me to say that she was watching 3ABN and saw something about

Wildwood. She said she knew I didn't like it but wouldn't I reconsider going there. She thought it would be a good experience. It shocked me that she mentioned Wildwood, without knowing that I had already applied to go there.

When I arrived at Wildwood my dark clouds seemed to have no rainbow. Alison, you always said that I helped you in your healing process, that I supported you in your darkest hours. I was in darkness also. Thank you, my friend, for through your constant desire to honor God and stay faithful, you helped God answer the prayer that I prayed in a country far away from where you were. When I think about that, it is almost impossible for me to believe.

Johana's support continued to prove invaluable to me. On November 6 I had my second follow-up visit with Dr. Boren. I dreaded it. However, that morning I read in my devotions: "He desires His people to show by their lives the advantage of Christianity over worldliness. By His grace every provision has been made for us in all our transaction of business to demonstrate the superiority of heaven's principles over the principles of the world."[4] Wow! God wanted me to demonstrate to Dr. Boren the superiority of His ways over man's ways! What a privilege. What a responsibility.

Right before I had to leave for the appointment I felt extremely anxious and fearful. I grabbed Johana and asked her to pray with me. She did, right there in the Russian steam bath room! I felt comforted and strengthened. Colleen drove me to my appointment once again. She prayed with me before we left—both of us crying—as she thanked God for the amazing way in which He worked in my life. She pleaded, "Give us the right words to speak to be a witness to this wonderful doctor." A few days before, Colleen told me that perhaps this visit would be more for Dr. Boren than for me, since I felt so well. I decided to write him a thank you card and, at Colleen's suggestion, bought a copy of the wonderful book, *The Ministry of Healing*, to give to him. I also typed out a detailed description of the program that I followed, in case he wanted to see it. Colleen wrote him a letter inviting him to come as a professional observer for a complimentary lifestyle program at Wildwood.

This second visit took place in a different location than the previous one. We were surprised to see a painting by Seventh-day Adventist artist Nathan Greene hanging there. This beautiful painting shows Jesus in the operating room with His hand on the surgeon's shoulder, guiding his

4   White, *In Heavenly Places*, p. 316.

hands. The confirmation it gave me simply blew me away: just the night before I wrote in the thank you card to Dr. Boren how much I appreciated the fact that he didn't give up on me. "I believe God had His hand on you during my surgery." Seeing that painting in his waiting room assured me that Jesus had been right there in that operating room and that He would stay with me, every step of the way.

During the long wait to see Dr. Boren, we watched the other ladies coming in: some with no hair, wearing hats, and some who could hardly walk as a result of the chemotherapy they were obviously receiving. Colleen couldn't believe the stark contrast between the way they looked and the way I looked. "This confirms for me that you made the right decision to refuse treatment. I would love a glimpse behind the scenes to see how God placing you with Dr. Boren not only impacts your life and his, but how it could possibly impact every woman who will sit in this room in the future."

When we finally got to see Dr. Boren, it turned out to be the most positive visit I could have hoped for. His first words were, "You look great." I beamed at him. "I feel great!" He asked me what I had been doing, so I pulled out my program and gave it to him. Impressed, he approved of everything. "In fact, I don't think you could be doing anything more. Keep on doing what you're doing!" When he asked about the Russian steam bath, Colleen took the opportunity to invite him to Wildwood and gave him her letter. He seemed interested.

We spoke about further testing. "If you are feeling fine, I don't see any reason to do tests on you. Most of the tests are invasive, and whatever the results, I know you aren't going to change what you are already doing." I also refused a pelvic exam, and he did not pressure me.

Dr. Boren requested to see me every three months, not so much for my sake, but for his. His curiosity urged him to see how this would all play out. "I don't want you to just disappear. I would like to follow up with you. I give you my full support, seeing your commitment to still follow your health program four-and-a-half months after surgery."

I assured him, "My commitment stems from my belief that this is God's way and that it works."

Being a Christian himself, he believed that faith is important. Colleen asked him about the painting, and he said his partner bought it. "I believe it to be a comfort to our patients." Handing him the card and book, I explained what I wrote in the card and how much it meant for me to see the painting in his office. "Thank you for what you did for me during my surgery. I believe you saved my life."

As we left, Dr. Boren gave me a hug. Colleen and I walked out of there saying, "Wow!" I felt all my fear drain away. We were both close to tears at the evidence of God's blessings. Colleen smiled. "I feel privileged to be a witness of what God is doing in your life." I felt in awe as I recognized His hand in everything, and the way He continually reassured me of His love and care. His glory truly flooded my soul!

Chapter 12

Burdens and Blessings

**"The most trying experiences in the Christian's life
may be the most blessed."**

(Ellen White, *Our High Calling*, p. 324)

As my physical pain began to ease, and reality settled in, the mental battle intensified. I felt keenly the absence of my close family members throughout this whole experience. My Wildwood friends were wonderful, but at the end of the day they went home to their families, and I sat alone in my little apartment with my fears. I did not understand why God saw fit for me to go through this alone. Now I know He wanted to teach me the invaluable lesson that He is enough. He has proved Himself to me as my Savior, Provider, Protector, and Healer. He is my Heavenly Husband and my Prince of Peace. But it was a slow learning process.

I fought the fear that the health program I followed would not be enough, especially when people advised me as to what I should or shouldn't be doing. But then I reminded myself, "It's not about me and the things I am doing. It's all about God and His healing power." I trusted Him to show me if I needed to change anything. Colleen encouraged me, "Ask God to double or triple confirm everything He wants you to do." This He has done without fail. I rejoiced in how God confirmed His will for me. The biggest confirmation came after my decision to refuse radiation and chemotherapy. I stumbled across 2 Samuel 24:14: "But it is better to fall into the hand of the Lord (for his mercy is great) than into the hands of men." I almost jumped for joy! It described exactly what I had chosen to do and what peace it brought! It is interesting to me that I first had to take the leap of faith, and then the confirmation came.

My parents, even though far away in South Africa, were a rock of support for me. My mom e-mailed me every single day since the crisis began, and her words carried me through many difficult days. She advised me, "Don't listen to the lies of the enemy. Just thank God for your healing and rest in Him. He has placed His hand on you, and will not leave you to flounder as to whether He has healed you or not. His promises are sure, and there have been so many confirmations that have shown you and us that God has opened the way for healing for you." I confided to my mom that I hated being alone in my apartment because of the memories there of the suffering I went through. She suggested, "Why don't you rather look at it as being your sanctuary where you can be alone with God, and He will meet you there?" That changed my whole perspective and I learned to enjoy my little home once more.

How I longed to have an undaunted faith that would trust God, no matter what! As I leaned on their support, I learned to appreciate my parents in a far deeper way than I ever had before.

My children blessed me, too. Melissa talked with me often and encouraged me. One day as I battled the pain and fear, she sent me these wonderful words, "Just repose in Jesus. Rest in Him as a tired child rests in the arms of its mother. The Lord pities you. He loves you. The Lord's arms are beneath you. You have not reined yourself up to feel and to hear; but wounded and bruised, just repose and trust in God."[5]

I texted Kyle one morning and sent him a picture of myself with a bunch of flowers Ed had sent me. He texted me back, "Soooo pretty!!! Oh, and the flowers are really nice too." That made my day! Knowing that my son still loved me in spite of the mistakes I made as a mother comforted me. He inspired me, too: A few years before, at the age of eighteen, enduring the extremely stressful and difficult South African process of getting his driver's license, he stayed calm. The day he went for his driving test I felt more nervous than he did! He calmly reassured me, "Mom, failure is not an option." And it wasn't, for he passed with flying colors! When I had a difficult day, battling the fears, Kyle's words came back to me. I could move forward, for when I am in God's hands, failure is never an option!

---

5   White, *Daughters of God,* p. 221.

However, I struggled to accept the reality of my situation. My life wasn't supposed to turn out this way. I felt too young to die. I kept wishing that this could all be a dream and I could simply wake up and go back to the way I had been. I think I had to go through a grieving process for what I had lost. My body would never be the same again, with a huge scar down my middle. The hysterectomy threw me into menopause and I had to deal with the consequences of that. Losing a quarter of my body's lymph nodes severely compromised my immune system and put me at risk for swelling in my legs. And I would always have the "shadow" of cancer hanging over me. Being diagnosed with something so aggressive and extensive meant I would have to be extremely careful with my lifestyle for the rest of my life.

I didn't understand why this had happened to me. I always tried to be a good girl and live a healthy life. I may never know, fully, this side of eternity why God allowed this trial to come my way. There were only two possible explanations that I could come up with at the time for what caused my illness. Either all the unrelenting emotional pain and stress throughout my marriage and separation, and finally divorce, suppressed my immune system, or this was a direct attack from the enemy who wanted to destroy me. As Jesus said in Matthew 13:28, "An enemy has done this" (NKJV).

The enemy's attacks were relentless. Fear became my constant companion, and I ended each day absolutely exhausted from the mental battle. It felt worse than all the physical pain I suffered. The terrifying predictions of the doctors were burned into my brain and the only way to survive was to override them with the Word of God. Colleen pointed me to Isaiah 59:19, which says, "When the enemy comes in like a flood, the Spirit of the Lord will lift up a standard against him" (NKJV). I clung to that verse. Every morning I pleaded, "Jesus, I'm crawling into Your lap. Please wrap Your strong arms around me and hold me today. Give me Your perfect peace."

Walking outside became one of my greatest blessings in dealing with the fear. When the enemy tormented me with scary thoughts I fled outside and walked and pleaded, "Lord, take control of my mind. Don't let me spiral down into that fearful pit of despair." Walking always made me feel better. I felt that if I had the strength to be up and walking I must be all right. I begged the Lord often on my walks, "Please, no more hospitals and doctors—please, can I just be OK now?"

God spoke to me through nature. One gorgeous Sabbath morning I went out for a walk just as the sun came up. The sky over the Lifestyle Center became a striking palette of pink and orange. I stood and admired it for a few moments. Then, as I turned to face the other direction, there in the pink clouds shone a beautiful rainbow! It had not been raining, and I had never seen a sunrise rainbow before. I felt that I had been given a special gift from God—a promise that He would always be with me and that He would heal me. I believe God does a special work of healing in our lives on the Sabbath day, as we take the time to rest in Him. I will never forget my Sabbath rainbow.

I struggled with not eating 100% raw, as my background with the raw food diet had given me the mentality that 100% raw is best. However, Dr. N insisted I needed to be balanced, and have some cooked grains and legumes. I struggled with eating fruit, even though Dr. N assured me that fruit is good. Many people warned me that fruit is sugar and you need to stay away from it if you have cancer. It didn't make sense to me though, because fruit is the food God provided as the ideal diet for man and is healing for our bodies.

But God patiently reassured me over and over again, until I made peace with the path He gave me. He allowed me to come across a number of articles on different fruits that are good for cancer, like peaches, pineapples, kiwis, and berries. I reasoned that if those fruits can be cancer-fighters, then why not all the fruits that God created? He told me, "Stop listening to teaching that contradicts what you know is right" (Proverbs 19:27). I recently decided to conduct an experiment and googled every fruit I could think of in connection with cancer. What a thrill to find that every single search brought up article after research article talking about how that particular fruit kills cancer cells! I feel as though I want to be God's champion for fruit!

When tormented by the fear of eating honey, God led me to these verses: "Eat honey, my son, because it is good" (Proverbs 24:13, GW). "His diet consisted of locusts and wild honey" (Matthew 3:4, GW). "So they gave Him a piece of a broiled fish and

> *The enemy still tries to bring these fears back to me on a regular basis. I have to give them to God every time and trust Him with my healing.*

some honeycomb" (Luke 24:42, NKJV). A disclaimer here: I don't eat honey often, and when I do, I make sure that it is raw, unprocessed honey. But I now can enjoy a little without feeling fear that it's going to kill me!

Dr. N stressed the importance of enjoying my food, because when I do, it releases dopamine in my brain. This is the happy chemical that helps in the healing process. She also told me to do things I enjoyed, like playing the piano. This all contributes to the positive mental attitude so necessary for healing. The enemy still tries to bring these fears back to me on a regular basis. I have to give them to God every time and trust Him with my healing. He shows me every step of the way what I need to do, and I have to believe that He will continue to do that.

The following quote helped me to make peace with my food: "Some are continually anxious lest their food, however simple and healthful, may hurt them. To these let me say, Do not think that your food will injure you; do not think about it at all. Eat according to your best judgment; and when you have asked the Lord to bless the food for the strengthening of your body, believe that He hears your prayer, and be at rest."[6]

During a follow-up appointment, I shared with Dr. N the spiritual battle I experienced on a daily basis. I told her about the verses of Scripture that God had given me, and how He sent encouragement to me in so many ways. Her eyes filled with tears. "You are a beautiful woman, and I see Christ in you." This startled me. I felt so weak. She assured me how much I had blessed her with the hydrotherapy and massage treatments during her first days at Wildwood. It humbled me to think that God somehow revealed Himself to others through me. I felt unworthy. In my mind, *Dr. N* was the beautiful woman who reflected Christ to *me*.

In a much later visit with her, Dr. N gave me a glimpse into how much she had depended upon God to guide her in my treatment. As we discussed the early days after my surgery, she admitted, "We were both scared." I am thankful that I had no inkling of her struggle, for she only ever calmed my fears with her confidence and God-inspired wisdom.

I learned how to take my fears to God. Experience taught me that whenever I cried out to Him, He gave me His peace that passes all understanding. I became better at turning my fears over to Him as soon as the enemy attacked. I don't know how many times a day I reassured myself, "You're OK, you're OK." Or, I repeated Dory's line from *Finding Nemo*: "Just keep swimming!"

A blessing that I am thankful for is that in spite of the fear that stalked me relentlessly by day, I never felt afraid to go to sleep at night. I felt safe in my bed and God gave me a peace that I cannot explain. The fears did not bother me and my sleep would be sweet. What a gift! Every morning when I opened my eyes I prayed for three things, and I still do! I ask for healing—physical, emotional and spiritual; wisdom to know how God wants me to cooperate with Him in my healing; and peace of mind. He never fails to answer that prayer.

---

6   White, *The Ministry of Healing*, p. 321.

It gave me great comfort to know that those closest to me had peace about my situation. My parents believed that God had healed me, and assured me, "When God does something, He does it well and He does it completely. When He is finished, it is done!" Melissa confirmed, "I have peace about you, Mom. I know you are going to be OK." Kyle recently admitted, "Mom, when I heard your diagnosis, I told all my friends I knew you were going to be OK." My sister, Jenny, told me that when she and Richard heard about me, they felt a peace that I would be all right. "I believe all your emotional pain was cut out with that cancer and God is healing you completely."

There were three Bible verses that became filled with meaning for me. The first was the one my pastor friend in South Africa gave me when he heard my diagnosis: "I will give you back your health again and heal your wounds" (Jeremiah 30:17). I clung to that promise with every fiber of my being. My physical wounds were great, but an even greater blessing has been the healing of my emotional wounds. I kept asking God to give me another verse to confirm His promise of healing to me. Over and over again, He reminded me of this fact: "He is the God who keeps every promise" (Psalm 146:6). One promise is enough, for He always keeps His word!

The second verse I claim is written on a plaque that a friend gave me for my birthday, just a few short weeks before my life changed forever: "For we walk by faith, not by sight" (2 Corinthians 5:7, NKJV). Choosing to step out in faith and trust my Heavenly Father with my healing, instead of the medical profession, was the scariest thing I've ever had to do. The enemy challenges me on this every single day.

The third verse is one that God gave me during my devotional time one morning: "Behold, I am the Lord, the God of all flesh. Is there anything too hard for Me" (Jeremiah 32:27, NKJV)? What a blessing to know that my God is a God who delights in impossibilities! "God invites us to prove for ourselves the reality of His word, the truth of His promises ... His promises will be fulfilled. They have never failed; they never can fail."[7]

He never fails to speak to me through His Word. Countless times during this dark season of fear and uncertainty I opened my devotional and started crying as I read words that spoke directly to my need that day. One morning in August I pleaded with God, "Please help me to leave behind the trauma of the surgery and everything that has happened to me. Please speak to me through Your Word today." This is the verse He gave me: "Forget the former things; do not dwell on the past. See, I am doing a new thing! Now it springs up; do you not perceive it? I am making a way

---

7   White, *Steps to Christ*, p. 111.

in the wilderness and streams in the wasteland" (Isaiah 43:18, 19, NIV). His Word has become so real and personal to me! It is the voice of God to my soul!

On August 18, 2015, Melissa messaged me and asked if I could Skype with her. I knew something was afoot because the sun had barely peeped over the horizon in Canada. Melissa and Daniel were both on the call and they shared with awe and excitement, "We're going to have a baby!" Melissa confided to me much later that they weren't planning to have a baby quite so soon. But after what had happened to me, they decided to get pregnant, in the hope that it would bring joy into our lives and give us something to look forward to. I rejoiced with them, but the enemy kept pushing the thought, "Am I even going to get to see this baby? I don't even know if I'm going to see next month." I tried to hide it from Melissa and Daniel but after we finished the call, I cried bitterly. I feared that my life was over and I would never share the joy of my first, precious grandchild's arrival.

A few days later I faced what felt like an overwhelming challenge. Trevor informed me that I needed to go back to working full time. My religious work visa required me to work in hydro and Wildwood had already given me as much of a grace period as they dared. But I feared that I did not have the strength yet, and that it would compromise my health. The work in hydro is physically taxing, as well as emotionally draining. I did not feel ready for either. At times like this my life seemed too much to handle. Tired of fighting the battle on my own and trying to be strong, I longed for someone to take care of me. I had an oppressive foreboding that I didn't fit in anywhere anymore, that people didn't quite know what to do with me. Everything seemed so uncertain. I wanted to get back to "normal," but I had a hard time believing in the future. I prayed desperately for peace of mind.

However, going back to work full time turned out to be the best thing for me. I returned to my routine of working mornings in hydro and afternoons in the Guest Services office. I felt happy to be back in hydro, working side-by-side with my special friend, Johana. My supervisor, Auntie Sara, treated me with compassion and allowed me to transition slowly into carrying a full work load again. To my surprise, I found that I managed just fine. Being back at work gave me a sense of normalcy, and I felt more capable and confident in myself.

One night, shortly after going back to work in hydro, I had a beautiful dream. I don't usually remember my dreams, but this one stayed with me and made my heart sing. I dreamed I flew through the sky, right up to heaven. I felt an indescribable joy. I saw the Ten Commandments written in huge letters in the sky, and in my dream I shouted at the top of my voice, "I love you Jesus!" The morning after that dream I had an amazing experience in hydro. Johana and I were scheduled to give a fever treatment to a patient with colon cancer.

Fever therapy, or hyperthermia treatment, is an intense treatment given by two therapists, and can take up to two hours or longer. It involves submerging the patient in a tub of water and inducing a fever by raising the temperature of the water. The patient's head is kept cool with ice water, and their vital signs are checked every five minutes. Holding the fever for at least thirty minutes or more has the benefit of mobilizing the immune system radically. The patient's temperature must be returned to normal before being allowed to leave the tub.

I felt compassion for this precious woman, with my own experience still fresh in my mind. The after effects of my dream lingered, and my heart sang with joy as we gave the treatment. At one point we asked the patient how she felt, and she exclaimed, "I'm so happy I feel like singing! Do you know the song 'I Must Tell Jesus?'" Johana found the words on her phone but she didn't know the tune, so I sang it by myself—with all my heart! Those who know me would find that most unusual, as I don't like to sing by myself! Then I sang "Standing on the Promises" for her. We got to talking about our favorite Bible verses, and I shared with the patient the ones that had been so meaningful to me. The whole one-and-a-half hours became a blessed time of sharing.

I noticed Johana stayed kind of quiet. Puzzled, I later questioned, "Are you OK?" Johana smiled. "I am in awe of what I just witnessed. I know you are a shy, quiet person, but you were sharing with such confidence and conviction. I always tell you that I see God's power working in you, and that I know He has a special work for you to do. I saw evidence of that today. This is just the beginning. You have no idea of the adventures God is going to take you on! You made my day!"

I was dumbfounded. "I have no idea what happened. All I can say is I felt the Holy Spirit with me. I shared what I did because it has become so real to me and simply bubbled out of me. I couldn't help it!" I felt so privileged and humbled to see how God used my fiery trial to touch the life of another. I caught a glimpse that day of what His purpose for me at Wildwood could be. I would hate for anyone to think that I am being boastful in any way. I give God all the credit for what happened that day. He deserves the honor and glory. I love Him so much!

Ever since I arrived at Wildwood, Melissa and I talked about getting together. Since she could not leave Canada until her permanent residence was approved, I planned a trip to visit her. When I began talking with Ed in March of 2015, I had another reason to want to visit Canada! About two months before the crisis broke, we booked a plane ticket for a September visit. I applied for two weeks' vacation time, which the Personnel Committee approved. A few months later my sister Jenny and her family moved to the academy close to Melissa's home, and I had one more reason to visit. I think God knew I needed to have this trip planned and confirmed, as it became something that I held onto through the whole nightmare of my surgery and recovery.

However, as the day of my flight drew near, my feelings about making this trip were extremely ambivalent. I longed with all my heart to be with my daughter, with Ed, and with my sister. It had been devastating to go through this crisis without my family. On the other hand, on my darkest days, I doubted whether I would even live long enough to make the trip. Or, if I did live that long, it would be barely three months after my surgery and I didn't know if I would have the strength to make the long journey.

Contemplating this trip to Canada overwhelmed me. I had to travel alone; I didn't know what I would eat on my journey; I feared that I wouldn't be able to walk enough on the flights and that my legs would swell (or worse); and I feared that I wouldn't be able to follow my health program well enough while staying with Melissa. And I felt nervous about meeting Ed in person. But the desire to be with those I loved overrode all my fears and I simply had to go.

The trip turned out to be a wonderful, yet agonizing, part of my journey to recovery. God used it to do an amazing work of emotional healing in me. Being with Melissa and Daniel comforted my heart. They made me feel completely at home and Daniel remarked to me more than once, "It's so nice to have you here with us." I had a number of opportunities for heart-to-heart talks with Melissa and to cry with her. It felt like a weird kind of role-reversal to have her comforting me, but her encouragement played a huge part in my healing. Spending time with Jenny and Richard blessed me, as we shared with each other just like old times on the farm back in South Africa. We discussed how what should have been the best years of my life were consumed by stress and unhappiness. My spirits were lifted by a verse they shared with me: "And I will restore to you the years that the locust hath eaten" (Joel 2:25, KJV). What a wonderful promise to hold on to!

While in Canada, Melissa gave me a book documenting people who have survived cancer against all odds. I believe God put this book in my hands to encourage me. As I read through the stories of survivor after survivor, my hope grew and my faith in the path that God had shown me to follow strengthened.

Meeting Ed in Canada became the agonizing part of my visit, as I began to realize that this relationship might not work out. Getting to know someone over Skype and actually meeting in person are two different ball games. The pain cut deep, for this man had become a huge part of my life. As things with Ed unraveled, God taught me how to express my emotions through crying. All my life I found it difficult to cry. I felt things deeply but never seemed able to express it through tears. On rare occasions I could cry, but it never felt enough. I often wondered if there was something wrong with me, as other women seemed able to cry so easily.

Puzzling over this, I remember a time when my self-worth hit rock-bottom and I hated who I was, feeling that I didn't deserve to cry. When my emotional pain threatened to surface, I told myself, "Stop crying. You're just a baby. Pull yourself together." And I pushed the tears back down. This led to my illness I believe, as things stayed bottled up inside me and I couldn't experience the emotional healing that a good cry can give. I refused to allow myself to feel my pain or to cry, for I believed that I must be such a terrible person that even my own husband could not love me.

Somehow in Canada, God broke through that barrier inside me and a miracle happened. I took a walk alone one day in the forest, agonizing with God about all the terrible things that kept happening to me. I began to cry at the thought of losing Ed, and seemed to sense God saying to me, "It's OK, you can cry, you can let go—give it all to Me." I gave *all* my pain and fear to God—my hurts going right back to my childhood, the loss of Chrissie, the loss of my marriage, my anguish and fear and grief at the loss of my health and my body that would never be the same again. The more I cried the more the sobs began to come from deep inside of me, until I felt as if my whole body would break apart. I don't know how long I cried but afterwards I felt completely exhausted and yet completely at peace. I committed myself into God's hands. "Do whatever You want with me. I am your girl and You are my only hope." I think I cried more that day then I had my whole life previous to that!

This experience began my emotional healing, and I am in awe of what God has done and is still doing to take me from brokenness to wholeness in every way. When we feel we cannot take another step, when human comfort is not enough, He will lift our heavy load and carry us. On days when I had no strength left to fight, He lifted me up and carried me. What a precious experience.

A few weeks after returning to Wildwood my friendship with Ed finally ended and I closed that chapter of my life. I remembered how much I prayed from the time I met Ed, asking God to intervene if this was not the right man for me. Now I accepted that He had given, and He had taken away, and I could still bless His name. God reassured me, "It's time to let Ed go. You are strong enough now to depend on Me alone. I am well able to meet all your needs."

After losing Ed, God drew me into an intimacy with Himself that I never dreamed possible. But it took a broken heart to open the way. Ed will always be a part of my story and I will never regret meeting him. As I realized that God wanted me to be at Wildwood for now, I embraced it. He gave me peace, contentment, and a love for my work that I did not have before.

Since leaving the hospital, my medical bills of close to $200,000 had weighed heavily on my mind. Having no way of paying these bills, I cried out to God for help. On October 6, 2015, I received a letter stating that my entire hospital bill of $110,000 had been written off—I had a *zero* balance! A number of people told me that it is unheard of for a hospital to write off their entire bill like that. Tears of relief flowed, and I felt awed that my God would do something so wonderful for me. One by one the other providers followed suit and wrote off their bills. Eventually the only bill that I ended up having to pay was a bill for $25 for an EKG I had in the hospital! In seven months God took care of that mountain of impossibility!

Continuing visits with Dr. Boren were positive and yet scary. As usual, Colleen accompanied me on these visits. I felt less nervous each time, but still hated going back into that environment with all the bad memories. I had to remind myself, "This is the man God used to save your life!" Every time I went back for a visit, I saw that he was unsure of what he would find—almost as if he held his breath as he walked into the consulting room. He so much wanted to see me succeed.

During my February 2016 appointment, Dr. Boren spoke extremely directly to me about what my prognosis should have been with the stage IV cancer I had. "When I saw you one month after surgery, I already expected the cancer to be back. The odds of living two years after diagnosis and surgery are *zero*, and even living one year beyond surgery is doubtful." But as Melissa told me way back when it all started, "He is not a prophet!" I stood before Dr. Boren at the eight-month mark with an excellent level of health, already exceeding his expectations. Dr. Boren mentioned that when he told the other surgeon, who had removed my adrenal gland, how well I was doing, he exclaimed, "It's a miracle!"

When I told him that I felt fine, he advised, "Great! Just keep doing what you're doing. I have no doubt in my mind that there are cancer cells in your body, but you are managing them with what you are doing." Perhaps God would beg to differ with him! I've had friends tell me that it's no big deal—*everyone* has cancer cells in their body! Colleen teased, "By now you probably have less cancer cells than me, since you're sticking so religiously to your program!" But nevertheless, his words scared me.

I think Dr. Boren had a hard time believing his eyes. When we stood up to take a picture, he wanted to check me over quickly, feeling the lymph nodes in my neck, pressing on my abdomen and my upper back, and checking my legs. I had no swelling or pain anywhere. When we were done he circled my condition on his form—no longer "endometrial cancer," but, "*history* of endometrial cancer" because "I see no evidence of cancer."

In spite of this, discussing my prognosis caused all my fears to come rushing in. The mental battle exhausted me and all I could do was hold on to Jesus until the storm passed.

In spite of this, discussing my prognosis caused all my fears to come rushing in. The mental battle exhausted me and all I could do was hold on to Jesus until the storm passed. I knew things would look brighter in the morning—they always did. I reached out to my friends at Wildwood, and they came to talk, walk, and spend time with me. Their care comforted me.

Chapter 13

Dr. N's Letter

**"You do not realize now what I am doing,
but you will [fully] understand it later."**

(John 13:7, AMP)

Dr. N entered my life at the perfect moment. I believe God orchestrated our meeting in hydro just a few short weeks before I found out I had cancer. And He orchestrated my first appointment with her on that fateful day when my life changed forever. For a brief window in time, this young physician had a profound impact on my life. I will be forever grateful for her encouragement.

I shared with Dr. N about my February 2016 visit with Dr. Boren, and his words, "The scientific side of me wants to say, 'What in the world are we doing?!' The other side of me wants to believe that this is possible." Dr. N responded with an e-mail that helped me to understand why God allowed this fiery trial in my life and why He chose to heal me only after surgery, and not before:

As a physician, I understand where Dr. Boren is coming from …
But here is where I am at peace. I know that you understand that
it was out of God's loving kindness that He directed the hands of
Dr. Boren to keep searching for tumor cells and keep cleaning

it out when he wanted to give up. It was God's loving kindness that empowered you with the strength to keep walking after surgery, with the pain, the discomfort, the sleepless nights, the lack of morning appetite. Over my few years of practicing medicine, I have seen my patients give up when it is too hard, when they do not want to get up out of bed anymore. I felt cruel after those initial visits asking you to please keep walking, please keep eating, please get out of bed, please start using the weights, please juice but only in addition to the large amounts of fruits and vegetables, especially when you had no appetite. But with every request I kept pleading with God to give you the strength to follow through. Because healing and the power to follow through come only from Him as you yield your will to His.

I can sleep at night because I know that you lean on God heavily. Darkest night notwithstanding, you lean on Him, and hear His still small voice. You have surrounded yourself with an army of mighty mothers in Israel that will not let go of the throne of Heaven on your behalf, encouraging you, and asking that angels be sent to your side each day to lift your eyes to the hills and their Creator, the Maker of Heaven and earth. Your faith is not in remedies, but in the God who knows what you need. You trust Him completely and obey what He asks of you. He can entrust you not only with the trial of the cancer, but He can entrust you with His complete healing.

But what gives me great confidence is that I am not entrusting your care to "chance" as most physicians may think you are doing. You are in the hands of the Master Physician, the greatest Physician, THE One from Whom all healing comes. He sees what you and I cannot see. He holds back seas. You can imagine how many water molecules there were in the Red Sea that had to be held up against God's own laws of gravity. Yet, it is nothing for God to do. He used the human agent of Moses to do that. He could have done it Himself, but He used the simple Moses He created, with His simple staff made from materials He created, lifted up by the hands He formed, to confound the wise. The Divine cooperated with the human that the human might see. He used Dr. Boren in this because, as much as God could have cured the cancer Himself without surgery, He desires our faith—even Dr. Boren's—to be built on Him and not just miracles.

Alison, God is the author of human anatomy and physiology. Dr. Boren and I were taught that anatomy and physiology were chance. God cared enough about Dr. Boren who studied the anatomy and physiology that God planned and designed, to not allow you to be healed without the surgery. I believe God wanted Dr. Boren and I to see with our own eyes (me by reading the operative reports) what the extent of the cancer cells were so that we would never once think that it was any human being's sole doing that saved your life.

Dr. Boren would be reminded that the skills of surgery that come by the intensive studying that he has done all his life came as a gift from a Creator. Surgery is grueling. The hot lamps giving light, the intense scrutiny of every corner of the body cavity to find where the cancer hides can be taxing on the eyes, the back, and the arms and fingers held steadily, not to mention the mind that at times seems to be working against the surgeon's body, yet he works swiftly to limit the time under anesthesia and limit the blood loss. That Dr. Boren faced such a daunting task placed him face to face with his dependence on the Creator, who knew every nook, cranny, and crevice of your body and dutifully guided his hand to keep searching until the job was complete. COMPLETE.

He may not recognize it fully yet, but every time he sees you, Dr. Boren has to face his frailty as a human being; he has to face the reality that he is neither omnipotent nor omniscient and there is only One who is. I believe that each time he goes home after your visits, he wrestles with God, whether he realizes it is God with whom he wrestles! Physicians who wrestle and then do as you do, and surrender to God, will find salvation in the hands of their Maker. I see this wrestling happen so often. Many realize the implications of surrender if there really is a Creator and instead will twist science apart from God to satisfy their questionings. Others, in searching the science, will see God's handiwork and submit. Therein they find what God drew them into this field to find: Him. And then if surrendered, they will help their patients find Him, too.

Alison, God has entrusted to you the awesome responsibility of bringing myself and Dr. Boren face to face with Him. In the close of this earth's history, lives are at stake, human lives. The devil is battling for each heart. The devil battles for the attention of your heart because he realizes how dangerous you are in the lives of Dr. Boren, myself, or any other physician or patient who would hear or read your story, because your story is the story of Christ. Because you make sinful, prideful physicians whose confidence lies in years of intense study and research and sacrifice of time and family, such as myself, look at Christ and realize it is in Him that our confidence must lie. And if we do submit to that realization, then we are compelled as you are to point others whom we come across to Him.

So I entreat you, cling to Him, surrender to Him daily. Do it because you abide in Him in response to His great demonstration of love on the cross even while we were yet sinners and let Him work through you because you, trembling on your knees, are more powerful than all the hosts of darkness.

I ask of you one more thing. Ask God to please show you how to point people in your book to Him, not to magic formulas such as "one ounce of exercise plus three parts water plus four parts sunshine." So many books are about how "this" plan and "that" plan works. How sad God must be when He who created these things is left out of the picture, or at best, is referred to as "some power outside of ourselves." Pray that the Holy Spirit would inspire you to write how He worked. Pray He would show you how exercise or water or fresh air is not just science, but that it is the design of The Greatest Scientist.

My prayers will keep lifting on your behalf because you and your faith are more precious than gold that perishes.

My love and immeasurable thankfulness for your demonstration of faith.

How I appreciated the way God used Dr. N to open my eyes to the bigger picture. Our suffering becomes easier to bear when we can see a purpose in it. Dr. N's time at Wildwood ended after only six months, but they were the most important six months for me. God used her to minister to me when I needed it most. His timing is perfect!

Chapter 14

Set Free

"They [the former tyrant masters] are dead, they shall not live and reappear; they are powerless ghosts."

(Isaiah 26:14, AMPC)

As I reflect on my incredible journey, I see how God helped me to face my fears one by one and overcome them. He truly wants us all to be free! Sometimes I find it hard to wrap my head around all that has happened to me. There were moments when I felt like yelling, "Stop the bus! I want to get off! I don't like this!" But my mom reminded me, "You don't want to do that. Jesus is the bus driver. You need to stay on the bus—it's the safest place to be!" Johana agreed, "Your mom is right. Don't get off the bus. Open the window a little bit, but don't get off the bus!" This journey is one that I cannot avoid. I have to stay on the bus till the very end. But God has opened the window slowly but surely, and I am breathing the sweet air of freedom from fear. Johana always told me, "You are shooting your ghosts one by one!"

Experience has taught me not to listen to my feelings. I notice that towards the end of the day, when I am tired, fear is more likely to overwhelm me. I have learned to say, "You'll feel better in the morning." And it's true, for "Great is his faithfulness; his loving-kindness begins afresh each day" (Lamentations 3:23). I am learning to trust that God does not give us a gift only to take it away again. Romans 11:29 says, "For God's gifts and his call can never be withdrawn; he will never go back on his promises." How His heart must be wounded at my lack of faith. He gave me the gift of healing and I need to rejoice in that gift.

Not long after I arrived at Wildwood, Colleen shared with me a collection of scripture songs. I fell in love with them and bought all three of the CDs. Little did Colleen realize what a blessing those scripture songs would be to me as I battled the fear after my surgery. I found a quiet stretch of road near my home, and every time I went walking I had my headphones on with those songs playing over and over. I sang along and prayed and cried and worshiped. What healing God brought to my soul through His Word in song. I could not go walking, or take a nap, or be alone, without my music, for the fear overwhelmed me. Have you ever found that when you speak something out loud it is impossible to think about anything else? When we speak God's Word (or sing it in my case) we override the fearful and negative thoughts that the enemy tries to place in our minds. Listening to scripture songs constantly became my spiritual armor, and through it God enabled me to fight the enemy of fear, and to overcome. I am now able to take a walk without my music (although I still enjoy taking it along most of the time) and commune with God in the peace and quiet of nature.

The fear of the cancer returning haunted me every day and I clung to words of encouragement from any source. God never failed to send me comfort when I needed it. One day a former lifestyle guest called and I shared what had happened to me. Her words filled me with hope. "You are going to be fine. It's not coming back." She urged me to read Nahum 1:7, 9: "The Lord is good, A stronghold in the day of trouble; And He knows those who trust in Him … Affliction will not rise up a second time" (NKJV).

During a lifestyle program in February 2016, we received a number of ladies with cancer and I worked with one of them in hydro. Angela[8] had colon cancer that metastasized to her liver. A bleeding tumor made her extremely anemic. We shared much together and my heart went out to her. In sharing my story I find it hard to talk at length about myself. My introvert personality finds it strange! One day I told Angela that I talked too much, but she replied, "Not at all—I want to hear it all!"

Another day during her treatment she confided, "I'm so glad you're here." I had a flashback to myself a few months previous, lying on that bed and saying the same thing to Johana! If there's one thing I've learned, it's the vital importance of speaking hope and encouragement to those

---

8   Not her real name.

who are going through a crisis like this. We need all the help we can get! I battled my own fears all week, but God taught me to turn those over to Him. In opening up about my struggles to my patients I am encouraged and blessed by them. While sharing my fears with Angela, she startled me by observing, "You make people want to put their arms around you and protect you." I felt as though she had looked right into my soul.

My heart ached when I received the news that Angela passed away not long after she left Wildwood. It comforted me to know that she is resting in Jesus, for she always insisted, "Nobody can love me like Jesus can."

"K" was another patient who had a profound effect on my life. This singer/songwriter from Nashville, who fought colorectal cancer for over two years, avoiding medical intervention at all costs, intrigued me. She called herself a "wellness warrior" and I couldn't wait to meet her, as we were on the same journey. When she joined the lifestyle program I worked with her in hydro. We had an immediate connection, bonding closely within a few days. She wrestled with the decision as to whether or not to submit to radiation, as the tumor caused her tremendous pain. One day she had an amazing experience. I gave her a contrast shower and as the water pounded her body she agonized and prayed about what to do and the tears flowed. Suddenly she felt an arm around her shoulder, and thought, "Who's touching me?" It was so real and comforting and special to her that she didn't even tell me about it until much later. She felt as if God had reassured her, "Don't worry, I'm here. You don't have to make this decision alone." "K" didn't have a Bible, and so our chaplain gave her one. The first verse she opened to was Jeremiah 29:11, "For I know the plans I have for you."

"K" spent eighty-one days with us at Wildwood, and when she left we were both filled with hope that she would get well. However, about two months after leaving Wildwood, she passed away. I believe God was in control and He brought her to Wildwood at just the right time, for He knew what lay ahead for "K". In her own words, from a song she wrote about Wildwood: "This beautiful place has been blessed by God's grace; it's where I found Jesus again." God performed an amazing emotional and spiritual healing in her life during her time at Wildwood. He knew she needed Jesus more than she needed physical healing. I hope to meet her in Heaven one day.

After this experience, I wrote to my family: "I sometimes ask God why He has me working with cancer patients every day when my own experience is still so fresh. But maybe He is teaching me to face my fears and one day to overcome them. I struggle with fear each time one of my cancer patients loses their battle and wonder why God chose to spare my life and not theirs. I may never understand here on this earth—all I can do is choose to live each day in total surrender and consecration to the God who has done so much for me."

God constantly had to deal with my fears about eating. One day at lunchtime I overheard a lifestyle coach tell a cancer patient that she should be eating 75% raw. Immediately the enemy began pushing all my buttons again: "Am I eating 75% raw? Am I eating the right things? Am I OK?" I struggled to eat my lunch without fear. I prayed and asked God to help me have right thinking, then went and found Johana before I went back to work. When I confided to her my fear that I was doing something wrong with my diet, she exclaimed, "What are you worrying about? It's working isn't it?" I couldn't argue with that! I felt amazing! Johana had an incredible ability to put things in perspective. Time and again she chided me, "My friend, you are making a storm in a glass of water! You are OK, with a capital 'O'!"

I shared with my mom about my struggles with eating and she gave me further confirmation. "If we disobey His laws, then we cannot expect to have that full healing. But, I believe even then, when we occasionally fall into temptation, and eat something that we think is not so good, God does not strike us down with a disease. We underestimate God's understanding and compassion for us. If somehow we eat something wrong unawares, we must not fall apart. Satan loves to instill fear in us. This is the bondage he wants us to live under. But God says that the wisdom of the world is foolishness with Him. When God speaks, then IT IS FINISHED."

Praise the Lord He is infinitely patient with me. The more time passes and the reality sinks in that I am OK, the more I am thankful for the wonderful, healthy food God provides for me each day. I often exclaim to Him, "I love Your food!" When I find myself taking up once more the heavy burden of relying on myself and the things I am doing to stay well, God reminds me that it's not my efforts, but His power that is sustaining me. "God, who formed the wonderful structure of the body, will take special care to keep it in order, if men cooperate, instead of working at cross-purposes, with Him."[9]

When I find myself taking up once more the heavy burden of relying on myself and the things I am doing to stay well, God reminds me that it's not my efforts, but His power that is sustaining me.

9   White, Our High Calling, p. 267.

Philippians 1:6 says, "I am convinced and confident of this very thing, that He who has begun a good work in you will [continue to] perfect and complete it until the day of Christ Jesus [the time of His return]" (AMP). I cling to the promise that God will finish that work of healing which He began in me.

One day I came to the astounding realization that I am free from emotional eating! For most of my life I battled with eating when happy, eating when sad, eating too much, eating the wrong things. I prayed many years for deliverance from this. Finally I feel free! I know that for the rest of my life I have to be careful with the way I eat. But I am so grateful to God for restoring my health that I am happy to eat this way, and now find it easy. "Loving God means doing what he tells us to do, and really, that isn't hard at all" (1 John 5:3). I finally, fully embraced the health message that I heard about all my life. I will never touch sugar or an animal product again, and I have no desire to. For someone who used to be a chocoholic, that is amazing to me! When God sets us free He does a thorough job!

God also set me free from my fear of travelling. On April 20, 2016, my little grandson, Wesley Daniel, was born! I travelled to Canada a few days later to meet him for the first time. I felt nervous about making the long trip again, but knew that my body had grown stronger since my last visit. Every time I left my comfort zone at Wildwood to travel, I struggled with the fear of dying. The words of Dr. Boren during one of my follow-up visits were burned into my brain: "What you had was so aggressive that you cannot afford to deviate from your program for even one week." When I travelled I worried that I wouldn't be able to have the vegetable juices or the large quantities of raw foods that Wildwood provided for me. I feared that I wouldn't be able to exercise as much as I usually did. But then I reminded myself again that it is God's power that is sustaining me and keeping me healthy. As long as I am doing my best to take care of my body in whatever circumstances I am in, He will not forsake me. It is my faith in God's healing power that has made me well—not my efforts to follow a health program perfectly.

God promised me before I left: "It is the Lord who goes before you; He will be with you. He will not fail you or abandon you. Do not fear or be dismayed" (Deuteronomy 31:8, AMP). And He stayed true to His promise. God gave me an amazing peace throughout the whole journey to Canada and back and everything went smoothly. How blessed I felt to be alive and to meet little Wesley! Being with my loved ones did more for my healing than any strict adherence to my health program.

Chapter 15

Celebrating Life

**"He happily rejoices over you, renews you with his love,
and celebrates over you with shouts of joy."**

(Zephaniah 3:17, GW)

As the one-year anniversary of my surgery drew near, I reflected on the ups and downs of the past months. Through it all my Jesus had revealed Himself to me in countless personal and intimate ways. My heart thrilled with joy at the wonder of it all. I felt privileged to be His princess.

On April 2, 2016, I celebrated my 50th birthday—a birthday that I hadn't expected to see. My children blessed me with their messages on Facebook. Kyle wrote, "This woman is an inspiration to me. I'm her number one fan ... hands down! Love you Mom!" And Melissa posted, "I could not be more proud of, and thankful for, my brave Mom as she celebrates a new year of life! God has done unbelievable things for her this year—she is truly a walking miracle! Happy Birthday, Mom!" My mom's e-mail touched me: "You are so special to us. We can only say that God had this special plan for you all your life. He saw in you the treasures He can use for His glory. God has allowed you to go through many trials to refine you and bring out what He wants you to be, His witness."

However, it seemed as though the weeks prior to my surgery anniversary had been a round of one goodbye after another. Eventually I asked

God, "Do I have to be separated from everyone that I'm close to?" Perhaps He knew that I now had strength enough to lean on Him and Him alone. Maybe He planned to bring new friends into my life. I wasn't sure. Before I travelled to Canada to meet my grandbaby, Wesley, I had to say goodbye to Colleen and Trevor, as they moved on to new opportunities. Psalm 68:6 says, "God places lonely people in families" (GW). From the day I arrived at Wildwood, Colleen and Trevor welcomed me into their family and were my support and strength through the roller-coaster of the following two-and-a-half years. Colleen had been (and always will be) my "sister" in the truest sense of the word. There are no words that can express my appreciation to them. Wildwood did not feel the same without them.

Another sad farewell came as I left Canada after my two-week visit with Melissa and Daniel and Wesley. I had a wonderful time with them and got so attached to that baby! The tears flowed as Melissa and I hugged goodbye. I missed them terribly, but tried not to think about it too much, otherwise I would have been crying constantly!

In June my heart ached as I said goodbye to my precious Johana, who returned to Argentina. She had been an amazing source of strength and comfort and encouragement to me throughout the past year. A gift from God, she will forever be a part of my story.

But on a happier note, with His perfect timing, God gave me the gift of a visit from my son! Kyle came from South Africa just after Johana left, and we had two wonderful weeks together! It was an emotional time for me, as we had not seen each other since Melissa's wedding. How I had longed for his presence through the nightmare of the past year.

As I looked back I marveled. What a different woman I had become. I had peace and contentment. I had joy and self-confidence, for I knew without a doubt that the King of the universe loved me! I had purpose and fulfillment in my work. I saw God's healing power at work in me—physically, emotionally, and spiritually. He promised me that He would restore my health and heal my wounds, and He always keeps His promises!

One morning a verse that I read during my worship time intrigued me. "And the Lord spoke to me, saying, 'You have circled this mountain long enough; turn northward'" (Deuteronomy 2:2–3, AMP). I asked Him if He was about to bring some big changes in my life, or if this applied to my fears. In the last few weeks leading up to my surgery anniversary I noticed how my fears had significantly faded and how God had set me free. I remembered saying to myself a few months after my surgery, "If I can just make it to one year, I think I will believe that I'm going to be OK."

One year had passed and as I looked back, I saw how far God brought me in overcoming my fears. The bad memories of the suffering were fading. I rejoiced in my freedom!

Soon after, I had a follow-up appointment with Dr. Boren. I could face it with courage, knowing that God would be with me. In my morning devotions He said to me: "Jehovah himself is caring for you! He is your defender" (Psalm 121:5). "For your Maker is your bridegroom, his name, GOD-of-the-Angel-Armies! Your Redeemer is The Holy of Israel, known as God of the whole earth" (Isaiah 54:5, MSG).

As usual, I had a positive visit with Dr. Boren. I gained four pounds since I saw him last—exactly what I wanted, just to prove to him that I *can* gain weight! He explained, "When you have extensive cancer your body tries to deal with it by starving it, but in the process you starve to death. The cancer eventually takes over your metabolism and it is impossible to gain weight." The fact that I am able to gain weight is a good sign, and Dr. Boren was pleased. He went through the list of symptoms again and did a brief physical examination. Finding no problems whatsoever, he remarked, "I believe one hundred percent that the health program you are following is the reason you are alive and well. You may very well not have a single viable cancer cell in your body!" That made me smile, as I remembered one of my earliest appointments with him when he told me he had no doubt that I still had cancer cells in my body! Dr. Boren tells my story to many people—even his oncology doctor friends. "Most of them don't believe me and tell me that the pathology must have been wrong. But I know what I saw inside you!"

When I insisted that it is God who has been so good to me, Dr. Boren recognized my journey and that it's important to give God glory. "But I find it incomprehensible that you could refuse treatment and manage to stick so determinedly to the path you chose. I understand that you didn't make your choice blindly. You made an informed decision. Most people just follow whatever the doctor says, no matter what they believe, but you chose to say, 'Thank you, but no thanks!'" He shook his head, "It's like jumping out into space trusting that the bridge will be there." I don't find it incomprehensible. I'm simply trying to stay alive and my God is the only One I trust! I shared with Dr. Boren for the first time about my mom's cancer, and Chrissie, and how God brought me to Wildwood. "I believe God prepared me my whole life for the choice that I made."

I thanked him again for what he did for me. "My Wildwood doctor told me how other surgeons, seeing what you saw, would have closed me back up and left me. For you to stand there for eight hours doing what you did for me, is amazing." He replied, "I was just doing my job." But I know God impressed him to do more than his job!

We had a beautiful sermon on faith in church the following Sabbath, and the pastor read a quote that made me think of Dr. Boren and his doctor friends:

> Men of science claim that there can be no real answer to prayer; that this would be a violation of law, a miracle, and that miracles have no existence. The universe, say they, is governed by fixed laws, and God Himself does nothing contrary to these laws ... Such teaching is opposed to the testimony of the Scriptures. Were not miracles wrought by Christ and His apostles? The same compassionate Savior lives today, and He is as willing to listen to the prayer of faith as when He walked visibly among men. The natural cooperates with the supernatural. It is a part of God's plan to grant us, in answer to the prayer of faith, that which He would not bestow did we not thus ask.[10]

That last sentence jumped out at me. I ask God every day to help me hold on to my faith and not to let Him down. He has done such wonderful things for me and I want my life to honor Him—to be a love letter to the world of how amazing He is!

---

10   White, *The Great Controversy*, p. 525.

Chapter 16

Twice as Much

"To give them beauty for ashes, The oil of joy for mourning."

(Isaiah, 61:3, NKJV)

As I write, it has been two years since my surgery. After being given only six months to live, that is nothing short of a miracle. A new me was "born" two years ago, on the night of my surgery, and that date will always be a celebration of life for me. At my two-year checkup with Dr. Boren, he exclaimed, "Every time you walk through this door you are a miracle!" Usually, if there is going to be a recurrence with his patients who have chemo and radiation, it happens within that two-year period. With the aggressive cancer I had, reaching the two-year mark with the level of health I am experiencing is a huge milestone.

However, the enemy still loves to push my buttons before every visit with Dr. Boren. I always have some minor physical problem that scares me, an odd little ache or pain perhaps, or just feeling lower energy levels than usual. Even though I have come to expect it, it still rattles me. But God is merciful and does not leave me floundering. Once I can find an explanation for my pains, I am able to relax and always feel fine by the time I go for the appointment. But I know that even if I can't find an explanation, I have to simply cling to God's promises and trust that I am safe in His hands. He has told me, "I want you to trust me in your times of trouble, so I can rescue you and you can give me glory" (Psalm 50:15). It's a slow learning process! Why can't I just believe Him when He says, "Daughter, your faith has made you well; go in peace, healed of your disease" (Mark 5:34).

I continue to experience God's loving care, and He keeps taking my breath away with the things He does for me! I feel undeserving of all the blessings, yet He continues to shower them down in spite of my human frailty and the many ways I fail Him every day. He is so precious to me! In Malachi chapter 3:10 and 12 He says: "I will open up the windows of heaven for you and pour out a blessing so great you won't have room enough to take it in! Try it! Let Me prove it to you!... And all nations will call you blessed, for you will be a land sparkling with happiness. These are the promises of the Lord Almighty." I have had to lean on Him heavily and He never lets me down. I truly feel as though I am sparkling with happiness!

> *I continue to experience God's loving care, and He keeps taking my breath away with the things He does for me!*

One day recently I got chills as I remembered my New Year's resolution at the beginning of 2015. I only made one, a prayer: "Lord, this year I want to have a closer walk with You and know You more intimately." He took that resolution seriously and answered my prayer in a way I would never have chosen, but that gave me the desire of my heart. All I could do was hold on for the ride!

People often ask me if I have had any tests or scans to prove that the cancer is gone. Dr. Boren periodically mentions the possibility of doing a PET scan, for curiosity sake. He puts no pressure on me, however, and says that it is not necessary from my health point of view, for he knows that I am fine. "I know what I saw. This woman should have been dead within six months, not alive and thriving!" When the subject first came up, I agonized with God over whether or not to do a PET scan. A number of people told me that it would make my testimony more credible if I had a scan to back it up, and I could not deny that. But I hesitated to do it, as I did not want to subject my body to anything harmful. And perhaps deep down I feared what they would find. I felt ashamed that perhaps I didn't really believe God had healed me and that my faith was weak. I knew that if God wanted me to do this, then I needed to face my fears and do it. I wrestled with God for a few days. Eventually I came to a point of surrender and told God, "I will do it if You want me to. But if You don't want me to, then please confirm that for me."

I asked my family and friends to help me pray about this. The following morning my mom and dad sent an e-mail: "It would be great to have this confirmation in your book. But are we not doubting God's hand? Hebrews 11:1 says that faith is the evidence of things *not seen*. You are not lacking in faith; all along you have trusted God. Your very life is witness enough to prove the validity of your book. Isn't true faith believing without seeing with your physical eyes that you are healed? God has the final answer. His Word will lead you and convict you without doubt."

The thought struck me that maybe it showed a lack of faith to put my body at risk and have the scan instead of trusting in God's promises. I knew that a previous Wildwood doctor told one of the cancer patients that PET scans are so dangerous that a person should not have more than three in their lifetime.

Melissa texted me: "I think arguments could easily be made for both sides, and that in the end it just needs to be what God tells you to do." Both Colleen and my friend, Anelize, told me not to do anything unless I have perfect peace about it. And Johana texted: "The Lord will be clear. Remember God is not a God of fear and confusion."

I went to bed that night pleading with God to confirm His will for me. Praise the Lord, I woke up to three confirmations the next morning that I did not need to do the scan. I had perfect peace about it. The first confirmation came from my brother-in-law, Richard: "Don't let this stress you in any way. Just be still and let Jesus move on your heart. Since it is really so bad I would choose not to do the scan but ask the Lord to inspire you otherwise if He sees fit. Make the best decision for your body but allow Him to move you if His will is different."

The second confirmation came from my mom and dad: "Is your book going to be one of proving the medical world wrong, or is it how much you clung to God, the miracle of how He brought you through, and your stand on using natural remedies? You know you are living proof of His healing power. All glory must go to God, for our loving Father spared your life miraculously. To me the miracles He performed right through your whole experience is where the power of your message to others lies. God's glory, God's power, God's love and care for you."

And the third confirmation came from Johana:

God will give you peace about this decision. I work in ICU with doctors and oncologists and cancer patients. I know how these doctors think. A scan would give specific proof of God's miracle. But as a Christian, I see something more. Your surgeon saw the cancer, you had an eight-hour surgery, you have the pathology. There was no mistaken diagnosis. And you have the scars. There is no doubt you had cancer. It is a miracle you are alive. You have Dr. N's and Dr. Boren's testimony—you don't need any more proof. You can't see inside your body, but you and everyone else can see you are OK—and with your diagnosis, you weren't supposed to be OK. It is a complete miracle.

It was the same in Jesus' time, with the Pharisees asking for signs. Jesus told them, "Even if I performed a miracle for you, you still would not believe." It's not about the sign. A skeptic will remain a skeptic even if you put a scan in your book. I know doctors who will see your PET scan and still say maybe your diagnosis was mistaken, or call it a spontaneous remission … Your book is about honoring God. Remember, this is God's story, not the doctors' story. People that will truly be blessed by the book will believe your words, the doctor's testimony, and your documents that prove you were sick. They will believe by seeing you alive, sharing your story. Life is the best proof.

When I e-mailed Dr. N about my decision not to do the scan, she sent me the following e-mail:

So proud of you. You have learned what so many Christians fail to do when faced with trials. You have learned to take it to God and let Him decide. God knows He can speak and you will listen and discern between the many voices around you. That is what I admire about you, where I wish all my patients I have ever seen would be. For that matter where I wish I would consistently be.

I have been praying for you about this. I have refrained from responding about the PET scan so as not to influence your decision too unnecessarily just because I am a physician. As much as the curiosity is there in me because the physician mind craves something tangible like a PET scan, I have been reminded this week what Jesus told Thomas, "Thomas, because thou hast seen Me, thou hast believed: blessed are they that have not seen, and

yet have believed" (John 20:29, KJV). I do not believe that Bibli-
cally it is wrong for someone to want proof; at that time that was
what Thomas needed because his faith was weak. But how much
more, Christ says, if we believe with the evidence He has given us.
That is faith.

If you think you need to do this for Dr. Boren's sake, consider this.
Remember Abraham believed and it was counted to him for righ-
teousness before the work occurred, according to Romans. The
works followed though because it was sealed in his heart. God has
reached Dr. Boren's heart through your life of faith—it is sealed
in his heart. You know how I know? Because he has been willing
repeatedly to bill your diagnosis as "history of cancer." That is
a legal thing and most physicians would not put that down until
after year five. He also shares your story with his patients. And he
is willing to go on record in writing in a published book. His works
follow his faith. He really does not need the PET scan. He wants
to share with his colleagues and he knows that his colleagues have
been trained to not believe anything contrary to the current standard unless there is "irrefutable" evidence.

Dr. Boren was "up to his elbows" in cancer in your body. No one
needs to tell him what God has revealed to him and continues to
reveal to him every time you come through his door. Is it likely
challenging for him to sit in a room with his colleagues and make
them believe what he says is true? Sure. But that is not his job, that
is God's job. If God has convicted you to say no to the PET scan,
then nothing more that you do will help his colleagues come to the
light. If He felt that one of them would benefit from a "Thomas"
or "Gideon" experience, then He would have given you a defini-
tive answer other than the one you have received. It is not about
convincing them of no cancer; it never was the final endpoint. It
was about drawing you and those who would be touched directly
or otherwise by your testimony (myself included), to Christ, so
that they could overcome just as you did, by His blood.

How blessed I am to have precious people in my life who counsel me
through the difficult times. I am choosing to believe God's promises and
the evidence in my own body. At my two-year visit with Dr. Boren he asked
me again about the PET scan. "Are you curious?" I exclaimed, "No!" I
explained to him how I feel about it, that in my mind, having the scan is

like saying to God, "I don't really believe that You have healed me, so I'm going to do the scan to check." Right from the beginning I have chosen to walk by faith and not by sight. Dr. Boren nodded. "I totally understand. I should be the same way in my own life. I get it. Having a scan would be like second-guessing God. There is no need for you to compromise your beliefs simply for objective evidence."

As I consider my healing journey over the past two years, I see God's wisdom in impressing me not to have any scans. I believe going for a scan soon after surgery would have made me fearful and more likely to give in to the pressure of chemo and radiation. God's natural ways of healing are slow and my body needed time to heal. My part was to simply trust that what He had begun in me, He would finish.

God gave me one more confirmation just the other day, showing me clearly that it is not necessary for me to do a PET scan: "The living evidences of His power had been before them day after day, yet they asked for still another sign. Had this been given, they would have remained as unbelieving as before. If they were not convinced by what they had seen and heard, it was useless to show them more marvelous works. Unbelief will ever find excuse for doubt, and will reason away the most positive proof."[11] I rest my case!

Recently Dr. Boren arranged for me to have the genetic testing done for Lynch Syndrome. The result came back: "Positive—clinically significant mutation identified." In simple terms, our genes are like chapters in a book. My particular gene has about three pages of a chapter missing. This is significant, as other mutations might only be missing a sentence. It puts me at extremely high risk for colorectal, endometrial, ovarian, and gastric cancer, and elevated risk for pancreatic cancer, and explains why I had endometrial cancer at such a young age.

The other day I came across a couple of articles that talked about the cancer personality. To my amazement, it described me to a "T"! It helped me to understand how my personality and the way I handled stress contributed in a major way to the formation of cancer in my body, apart from the high risk associated with the Lynch Syndrome gene which I carry. An important realization for me was that I probably got sick because all my life I internalized my negative emotions. I didn't find it acceptable to express them, even when I had a right to—particularly anger when people hurt me. I had a poor self-image and tended to take the blame in conflict situations. Cancer patients who are able to face and work through their negative emotions are the ones who have a better chance of recovering.

11   White, *The Desire of Ages*, p. 386.

Most cancer patients have experienced a highly stressful damaging event in their lives about two years before their diagnosis. The situation comes as a "last straw" after years of suppressing their reactions to stress. This major stress suppresses their immune system and disease results.

Something that really worried me in one of the articles was the statement that the cancer personality finds it hard to forgive and forget. I believe this is related to the inability to express negative "unacceptable" emotions. I had to really ask God to search my heart, for as far as I could understand, I am not holding anything against anyone in my life. I have forgiven my husband and moved on. God gave me the opportunity, when I lived with my parents after my separation, to deal with my childhood issues and make peace with them. I pray often for God to search my heart and show me if there is any resentment, bitterness, unforgiveness, even self-hatred, there.

A few weeks later, God spoke to me clearly, "You need to forgive Me." The power and depth of this thought took me days to process! Perhaps somewhere deep down inside, I need to forgive Jesus for not preventing my suffering. If part

> *Perhaps somewhere deep down inside, I need to forgive Jesus for not preventing my suffering.*

of me believes that Jesus should have done something about it and didn't, then I have to let that go. I need Jesus more than I need to understand why these things happened to me. I don't want anything to get in the way of my knowing and loving Jesus in all His beauty. Learning to walk by faith and to trust all into the tender care of my Heavenly Husband is turning out to be the most precious experience of my life.

I understand now that suffering is necessary in our lives, and why God chose to heal me only after surgery and not before. The privilege of being comforted by God in my suffering had a purpose: "What a wonderful God we have—he is the Father of our Lord Jesus Christ, the source of every mercy, and the one who so wonderfully comforts and strengthens us in our hardships and trials. And why does he do this? So that when others are troubled, needing our sympathy and encouragement, we can pass on to them this same help and comfort God has given us. You can be sure that the more we undergo sufferings for Christ, the more he will shower us with His comfort and encouragement" (2 Corinthians 1:3–5).

As I contemplated the meaning of the story of Job, and how in the end God gave him twice as much as he had before, I thought, "What a wonderful ending for the book!" God spoke these thoughts to me: "You lost your blonde, blue-eyed little boy—I have given you a blonde, blue-eyed son-in-law and a blonde, blue-eyed grandson! You lost your health—I have made you twice as healthy as you were before—physically, emotionally and spiritually!" I ventured the question, "But I lost my husband, too. How can You give me two husbands?" Then He reminded me, "Jesus is your Heavenly Husband, and maybe someday He will share you with someone special!"

Many times I have asked the Lord: "Why me? I don't deserve life more than anyone else. I'm just a baby—how can I write a book?" This is what He says to me: "Before I formed thee in the belly I knew thee; and before thou camest forth out of the womb I sanctified thee ... Then said I, Ah, Lord God! behold I cannot speak: for I am a child. But the Lord said unto me, Say not, I am a child: for thou shalt go to all that I shall send thee, and whatsoever I command thee thou shalt speak ... Then the Lord put forth his hand, and touched my mouth. And the Lord said unto me, Behold, I have put my words in thy mouth" (Jeremiah 1:5, 6, 7, 9, KJV).

I cannot but speak the things which I have seen and heard and experienced (Acts 4:20). I consider it a great honor to be a testimony to the world of God's awesome power and His tender care for His children.

Jeremiah 18:4 says, "And the vessel that he made of clay was marred in the hand of the potter; so he made it again into another vessel, as it seemed good to the potter to make" (NKJV).

My life is marred. I have many scars. But how it comforts me to know that all these hurts happened to me while safely held in the hands of the Potter. And He is shaping me into something better.

I challenge you to prove Him! "Yet the Lord still waits for you to come to him so he can show you his love; he will conquer you to bless you, just as he said. For the Lord is faithful to his promises. Blessed are all those who wait for him to help them" (Isaiah 30:18). I rejoice in the gift of life and all the wonderful things God has done for me.

"Celebrate! Worship and recommit to God! No more worries about *this* enemy. This one is history. Close the books" (Nahum 1:15, MSG).

To Him be all the glory!

Two years old   *First day of school*

College graduation   *Chrissie*

With my children just days before Chrissie's diagnosis

With Kyle in Korea 2008

Mom & Dad

Jenny & Richard

*Melissa & I
on her wedding day*

Kyle & I at Melissa's wedding

First days at Wildwood February 2014

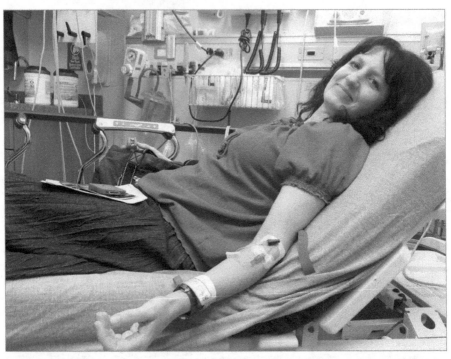

The nightmare begins June 8, 2015

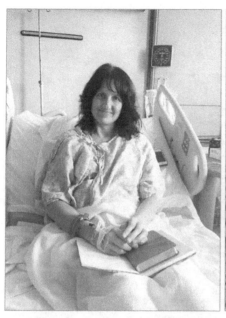

Day before surgery June 23, 2015

Johana

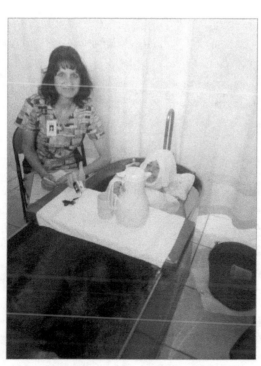

*Back to work a few months
after surgery*

Celebrating one year after surgery with Trevor, Colleen, Taryn, & Kyle

Colleen & I September 2016

Wesley

*Daniel, Melissa
& Wesley -
Twice as much!*

*Hydro girls
2017*

TEACH Services, Inc.
P U B L I S H I N G

We invite you to view the complete
selection of titles we publish at:
www.TEACHServices.com

We encourage you to write us
with your thoughts about this,
or any other book we publish at:
info@TEACHServices.com

TEACH Services' titles may be purchased in
bulk quantities for educational, fund-raising,
business, or promotional use.
bulksales@TEACHServices.com

Finally, if you are interested in seeing
your own book in print, please contact us at:
publishing@TEACHServices.com
We are happy to review your manuscript at no charge.

5/8 Alison

2 Samuel 24:14, Jer 30:17; 32:27; Ps 50:
Job 2:6; Is 59:19; Job 42:10; Luke 1:37; 2Cor 1:34

Recommended Readings: China The Study
                              Forks & Knives

CPSIA information can be obtained
at www.ICGtesting.com
Printed in the USA
FFHW010516281118
49663060-54078FF